Praise for *The New England Clam Shack Cookbook**

. . . **DELIGHTFUL READING** that eliminates the guesswork out of finding the best summer seafood shacks and houses and features many **SOUGHT-AFTER RECIPES**.

— Alice L. Bilello

Any cookbook authored by Brooke Dojny is going to be a favorite. **NO ONE KNOWS NEW ENGLAND CUISINE AS WELL.** This cookbook is one of her finest works.

— Karen Landry

I LOVE THIS BOOK! I'm already planning a clam bake . . .

— Lee Thomas

WHAT WONDERFUL AMERICANA! Makes me want to take a road trip to the New England area – and when I do, I'll know where to eat! This book is **PURE FUN AND INSPIRATION.**

— Nancy Ott

Greatly put together by Brooke Dojny . . . her suggestions were **RIGHT ON THE MONEY!**

— Dee Foerst

All comments submitted by readers of the 1st edition.

The NEW ENGLAND
CLAM SHACK
COOKBOOK

The mission of Storey Publishing is to serve our customers by publishing practical information that encourages personal independence in harmony with the environment.

Edited by Margaret Sutherland and Lizzie Stewart
Cover and text design of original edition by Wendy Palitz and Stephen Hughes;
   design modifications of second edition by Jessica Armstrong

Cover photograph by © Kindra Clineff
Illustrations by John Dykes except page 122, Maine Lobster Promotion Council
Photography credits appear on page 239

Indexed by Nancy D. Wood

Printed in Hong Kong by Elegance Printing
10 9 8 7 6 5 4

Library of Congress Cataloging-in-Publication Data

Dojny, Brooke.
   The New England clam shack cookbook / by Brooke Dojny. — 2nd ed.
      p.   cm.
   Includes index.
   ISBN 978-1-60342-026-6 (pbk. : alk. paper)
   1. Cookery (Seafood) 2. Cookery, American—New England style. I. Title.
TX747.D595 2008
641.6'92—dc22

                                                         2008004400

The NEW ENGLAND CLAM SHACK COOKBOOK

BROOKE DOJNY

2ND EDITION
Completely updated
with new restaurants
and travel plans
for eating around
New England

Foreword by
Susan Herrmann Loomis

Storey Publishing

To Susan Maloney,
good friend and clam shack connoisseur

I would like to especially thank and credit the 29 restaurant owners/chefs named in the restaurant descriptions, all of whom were so generous with their time, their expertise, and their recipes. Many people provided tips on their favorite "secret" clam shacks, lobster pounds, and chowder houses and shared knowledge of history and cooking techniques. Thank you to Skip Atwood, Dale Burmeister, Barney Butler, Debi Callan, Chowhound.com, Phyllis Corcoran, Peggy Coyne, Maryann and Dick Douglas, Jean Higgins, Steve Gertzof, Elinor Klivans, Barbara and Prescott Keyes, Keith Maloney, Connie McCreery, Sandy Oliver, Chris Schlesinger, Paul Skorupa, Jane and Michael Stern, Lee White, and Steve Woodman.

Thanks to all the people at Storey Publishing who worked on the first edition, most especially editor and primary creative force Dianne Cutillo. This time around, thank you to Pam Art and Dan Reynolds, and to Margaret Sutherland, who guided the project with good judgment and suggestions — and excellent clam shack radar. Jessica Armstrong art directed and added fabulous and fun visuals, and Lizzie Stewart did a great job of project editing, and Ilona Sherratt worked as the all-important illustration coordinator to get the new maps and other art in place.

As always, my agent, Judith Weber, did a masterful job. And I thank my husband, Richard, for sharing some of the fun (and acquiring, along with me, a bit of additional poundage) during the travel/research phase of the project.

Contents

Foreword

In *The New England Clam Shack Cookbook*, I take great pleasure from revisiting places and a culture I know and love so well. As I read through Brooke Dojny's friendly descriptions, I remember the sheer happiness of walking into a lobster pound and, amid the gurgling of the lobster tanks and the clanking of the boat rigging, choosing from among different items on the uniquely regional menu. I relive with her the delicious Portuguese-influenced seafood dishes in Massachusetts, the clear chowders of Connecticut and western Rhode Island, and the creamy rich chowders of Maine. I love the way she has unearthed contemporary dishes that play on tradition, too, like the stuffed quahogs of The Back Eddy in Westport, Massachusetts, and the mussel chowder at Thurston's in Bernard, Maine, with its sunny carrots and orange bell peppers.

You, too, will love Brooke Dojny's guidance during this delicious journey on New England's hidden roads and byways, which are replete with deciduous woods and

sea swells, bays dotted with lush islands, and charming characters. As you accompany her to the best clam shacks, lobster pounds, chowder houses, and out-of-the-way classic spots for sampling the finest seafood New England waters have to offer, you will feel the New England summer breezes riffle your hair, and you will smell the clear, clean, briny coastal air. What's more, on your return you will be able to prepare the foods you have just experienced, following the recipes that Brooke has gleaned from each establishment.

Perhaps even more than the recipes and homey locations in *The New England Clam Shack Cookbook* is the deep appreciation Brooke gives us for fragile seacoast traditions. Not one of the places in this book could exist without the strength and vitality of the New England fishing fleets and the courage, pride, and hard work demonstrated each time a skipper and a crew takes out a fishing boat or a diver suits up to go down under. Fishermen and -women are the backbone of the New England seaboard, the strength of its communities, the force that gives it its charm. By celebrating the food of this beautiful and abundant region, Brooke celebrates the industry that makes it all possible.

She further illuminates the region with informative sidebars intended to clarify certain New England mysteries, like that surrounding chowder (red, white, clear — which is the best?) and clam varieties. Upon reading this book, you will visit New England armed with plenty of inside knowledge!

The New England Clam Shack Cookbook will appeal to anyone who has ever been to New England, has dreamed of going, or has lived there for any length of time. Brooke Dojny has a warm corner in her soul for New England culinary and social traditions, and we must all thank her for sharing it in this delicious book!

— **SUSAN HERRMANN LOOMIS**
Author of *The Great American Seafood Cookbook* and *On Rue Tatin*

Traveling on My Stomach

Seafood, the jewel in New England's culinary crown, is nowhere showcased to more glorious advantage than in the informal, summer-only, eat-in-the-rough clam shacks and lobster pounds that are distributed over Yankee highways and byways, and in the year-round chowder houses that are institutions of long standing in New England's larger towns and urban areas. These straightforward, honest Yankee establishments carry the torch of culinary tradition by consistently serving up some of the very best food to be found anywhere in the United States.

Although these classic eateries have long been an established part of the New England landscape, the sad fact is that we can no longer necessarily take for granted that they are permanent and immutable. Developers press to gobble up plots of prime real estate that some of these establishments occupy. Family-run places may not have a member of the rising generation who can take over the operation. Trendiness exerts a force to be reckoned with.

These places, while undeniably humble, are glorious American institutions. They embody a legacy that I think should be acknowledged, encouraged, and supported.

My goal in writing this book was to search out the best of these eateries and record their histories, stories, and recipes. I traveled a couple of thousand miles, wending my way up and down the New England coastline, eating, tasting, assessing. When I found an establishment that I deemed book-worthy, I spoke with the owner and/or chef and requested recipes (a few declined to divulge their secrets). We then talked further about the history of their particular establishment. I listened to their personal stories and asked such questions as: How did you come to this work? Are other family members involved? What are the greatest challenges? What is most rewarding about it? During the course of this research I forged many friendships and gained a profound appreciation for the hard work and dedication required to run a successful clam shack, lobster pound, or chowder house.

The New England Clam Shack Cookbook is the result of that odyssey and of those friendships. Profiles of each featured restaurant are scattered throughout the chapters, and the 100-plus recipes in the book reproduce the way particular establishments make their own New England specialties. While they are an accurate reflection of the way these cooks make traditional Yankee dishes, the recipes are not meant to be the definitive last word on each and every dish.

For this, the second edition of *The New England Clam Shack Cookbook*, I logged another two thousand miles or so on the odometer, revisited most of my original picks, dropped a couple whose standards had slipped, and added several wonderful new establishments — and about 25 new recipes.

This is a personal book. Just as the recipes are not necessarily the last word on a dish, neither is my "top picks" list designed to exclude other worthy establishments or to be absolute gospel on the subject. Inevitably, I will have missed a few great ones. And there will no doubt be lively debate about my choices. Another caveat: While I've tried to give a general idea of when each restaurant is open for business, I recommend calling ahead to check on hours of operation. (And while you're on the phone, ask for directions. Some places are located well off the beaten track.)

My aim has been to celebrate the wonderful places that I found in my travels. If other people have favorite "secret" clam shacks, lobster pounds, and chowder houses — so much the better! Just add them to the list!

Happy clam shackin'!

OODMAN'S
EAT
THE ROUGH
ESSEX
CLAMS
IN THE SHELL
FRIED
CLAMS
LOBSTERS
LIVE
& BOILED

Welcome

CHAPTER 1

Clam Shacks, Lobster Pounds, and Chowder Houses Defined

Clam shacks, lobster pounds, and chowder houses in New England evolved quite independently from one another, so defining and differentiating these three types of delightfully informal New England eateries requires a few words of explanation.

Different historical factors were at play as each type of establishment evolved, and, although there is sometimes a bit of overlap — for instance, some lobster pounds also have indoor dining rooms and expanded chowder house–type menus — there remain distinct features that can be observed and delineated.

Additionally, so that travelers "from away" (as non-Mainers are called in the Pine Tree State) are prepared for the rather arcane procedures involved in "in-the-rough" ordering and eating, instruction and tips are offered.

Finally, I suggest many ways that you can use this book. Use it as a travel guide, leading you to some of the best meals you'll ever eat, or use it as a cookbook, sparking culinary adventures without leaving home.

Clam Shacks

According to legend, it was a hot July day in Essex, Massachusetts, in 1916 when Lawrence "Chubby" Woodman invented the first fried clam by rolling a shucked whole-belly soft-shell clam in some crumbs and immersing it in the cauldron of hot oil he used for frying his fried potato chips. Eureka! Not only was this a stroke of culinary genius, but Chubby's timing was also impeccable. The booming twenties were around the corner, Henry Ford was gearing up his automobile assembly line, roads were being improved and paved — in short, America was on the move. And as America moved, it wanted a little something good to eat, and it wanted that something to be fast, convenient, inexpensive, and kind of fun. And so, over the course of the next two or three decades, summer clam shacks were born, dotting the roadsides like little white mushrooms.

Capitalizing on more reliable electric refrigeration, the perfection of efficient commercial deep fryers, and, in the late 1920s, the invention of sliced bread, clam shacks developed a look, style, and menu that was uniquely their own. Usually family owned and run, and relying on high-quality ingredients cooked and presented with the utmost simplicity, clam shacks embodied the best of the American democratic spirit by encouraging folks from all walks of life to shed any pretensions and to step up to the window, place an order, and consume the quickly cooked food "in the rough," either sitting at a communal picnic table or perched on the hood of their car. Whole-belly fried clams and other fried seafood, top-loaded seafood rolls, baked stuffed clams, clam fritters, fish sandwiches, hot dogs, and hamburgers, with sides of fries, onion rings, creamy coleslaw, and sometimes ice cream or home-baked goods for dessert — these were the typical clam shack offerings back in the twenties, thirties, and forties, and they remain so today.

Lobster Pounds

Americans began to go lobster crazy in the early part of the nineteenth century, and as early as about 1850, special vessels outfitted with chambers filled with fresh seawater were plying the waters between Boston and Maine, carrying the perishable crustaceans to market. The fact that lobsters

HOW TO EAT IN THE ROUGH

Clam shacks and lobster pounds require that the customer be familiar with the informal "eat-in-the-rough" protocol. Here's the drill:

1. You stand at a counter or window and place your order, sometimes needing to yell it through all the commotion. At lobster pounds, you can specify the approximate poundage, and sometimes even choose the very live creature out of a tank.

2. The lobster is then stuck into a string bag — along with corn on the cob, steamers, or mussels, if you've ordered them — the bag goes in the cooker, and you sit down and wait until they call your name or number.

3. A few places have staff to deliver your meal, but usually you head back to the window to pick up your food, which will be presented on cardboard plates and with plastic forks.

4. Don your plastic bib and plan your attack. If you're a neophyte, watch a pro at a nearby table. Some pounds have "how-to" information printed on paper place mats. Lobsters from lobster pounds are almost always super fresh, right off the boat, and they're often boiled in seawater, which imparts additional flavor of the sea. All you need to add is a little melted butter for dipping — and maybe finish your feast with a slice of homemade pie — and you've found in-the-rough nirvana.

5. And don't forget to bus your trays.

had to be shipped alive meant that they needed to be impounded and kept alive while they waited to make the trip to market. Most of the earliest lobster "pounds" (the name is from the word *impoundment*) were constructed in coves with a narrow entry that could be gated to keep the creatures from escaping. As summer rusticators came to Maine in great numbers around the turn of the twentieth century, huge wood-fired cooking cauldrons were set up at the site of these coastal pounds so that visitors could buy their lobsters right from the source, watch them being cooked on the spot in the open air, and then settle down at an outdoor picnic table for a feast "in the rough." Now, of course, many pounds have moved inland along the tourist highways, but some remain in their original coastal locations — and many still have outdoor cookers, although most are fired these days with propane.

Chowder Houses

Capitalizing on the abundance of fresh seafood in New England, informal year-round seafood restaurants date back to the nineteenth century in the region. For well over a century, these eateries have maintained a consistent, distinctive look and style, usually involving cheerful highly varnished wooden walls and booths, mounted fish gracing the walls, and nautical ephemera scattered around the room. Carried forward today by a new generation of traditionalists, these restaurants offer a refreshing and welcome respite from the too-too trendy, the cutting edge, and the ultra-chic — and, of course, they serve up some of the wonderful New England classics that never go out of style.

While clam shacks and lobster pounds are usually summer-only seasonal operations, chowder houses, most of which are found in New England's larger towns and cities, are almost always year-round full-service restaurants. There are also establishments that fall somewhere in between — seasonal restaurants that offer full service. Most of these eateries serve much or all of the fare you can get at a clam shack or lobster pound, along with such other New England seafood specialties as chowders (clam, fish, and mixed seafood) and seafood stews, all manner of broiled and fried fish plates, including swordfish, haddock, and mixed fried seafood, and, of course, some fabulous classic Yankee desserts.

Instructions for Using this Book

- This is, first and foremost, a cookbook. Cook your way through it. And as you're eating the fruits of your labor, close your eyes and summon up a vision of New England summer. You're picking apart a freshly boiled lobster at a picnic table overlooking pine tree isles, scarfing down a scallop roll as you lounge in a beach chair, or, on a rain-swept day, slurping clam chowder while seated cozily in a varnished wooden booth. It's summer again, and all's right with the world.

- Treat it as a travel guide. Plan a trip around the featured restaurants and taste the food right at the source. It's not unrealistic to try to cover the entire route — from Lenny & Joe's Fish Tale in Connecticut to Thurston's Lobster Pound in Bernard, Maine — in a two-week trip. Carry a copy of this book, make notes on the pages (you have permission!), and ask restaurant owners to sign your copy. Then come home and re-create the dishes you've tasted and relive the experience all over again.

- Narrow your radius to a single state or geographic area and incorporate some of the other suggested restaurants in More Stops Along the Way (see pages 236 and 237), taking as much time as you have.

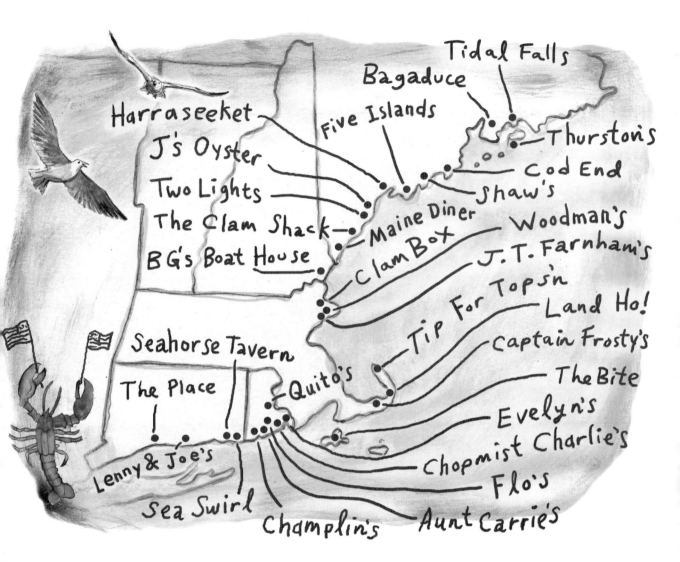

Tidal Falls

Bagaduce

Five Islands

Harraseeket

J's Oyster

Two Lights

The Clam Shack

BG's Boat House

Maine Diner

Clam Box

Thurston's

Cod End

Shaw's

Woodman's

J.T. Farnham's

Tip For Tops'n

Land Ho!

Captain Frosty's

The Bite

Evelyn's

Chopmist Charlie's

Flo's

Aunt Carrie's

Seahorse Tavern

The Place

Quito's

Lenny & Joe's

Sea Swirl

Champlin's

- Focus on one of the Weekend Itineraries and enjoy exploring a smaller piece of New England in depth. Use these recommendations or listen to local folks who might have equally good (or better) advice (see Ask — Then Eat — Local, page 103). Carry a copy of the book with you. Who knows? You might be offered a bit of special treatment!

- Use these recommendations as the starting point for creating a personal clam shack life list. After input from local sources, follow your nose and your instincts, and begin your own adventure.

CHAPTER 2

Snacks, Appetizers, and First Courses

Clam shacks aren't the kind of establishment you'd choose for a leisurely, full-course meal, but they are certainly an excellent choice when you're in the mood for a speedy, satisfying snack. If you're in Rhode Island or southern Massachusetts, what could be better than a quick stop at your favorite clam shack for an order of clam cakes (fritters), piping hot, fresh from the fryer, or a couple of well-spiced "stuffies"? At a lobster pound, enjoying an appetizer-type nibble while you wait can add to the agreeable experience of eating "in the rough." An order of local crabmeat spread or a big bowl of briny steamers with broth and butter for dipping is just the right way to munch away the 20 minutes or so of lobster-cooking time. And settling in for a relaxed, unhurried meal — one that you anticipate will include several courses — is part of the blissful, laid-back gratification of eating at a chowder house or other full-service restaurant. If you're snug in your seat at a chowder house, how could you go wrong with garlicky bacon-topped clams casino or cheese-sauce-napped oysters Mornay or, for the more daring gastronomes among you, a serving of herb-seasoned, vegetable-flecked snail salad?

Snail Salad

You see more Mediterranean-influenced dishes on menus in Rhode Island than anywhere else in New England, no doubt because of the large Italian and Portuguese populations that have lived in the state for generations. This snail salad is a delicious case in point. These are large sea snails — sometimes called *conch* — that are boiled and chilled, and the flavorful meat is thinly sliced.

4 cups thinly sliced cooked snail or conch (see Note)

½ cup olive oil

2 teaspoons mixed Italian herb blend

¼ cup finely diced carrots

¼ cup finely chopped celery

¼ cup finely chopped red onion

¼ cup finely chopped red bell pepper

2 teaspoons minced garlic

Salt and freshly ground black pepper

4 large Boston lettuce leaves

Lemon wedges

1. In a large bowl, combine the conch, olive oil, Italian herbs, carrots, celery, red onion, bell pepper, and garlic. Toss together and season with salt and pepper to taste. Refrigerate for several hours or overnight.

2. Spoon the salad onto a bed of lettuce, garnish with lemon wedges, and serve.

NOTE: Champlin's restaurant buys their conch in cans, already sliced, from Rome Seafood in Boston. Champlin's retail seafood market under the restaurant often sells whole cooked snails, which you should slice paper thin before using.

6 to 8 servings

Aunt Phyllis's Fabulous Famous Clam Fritters

Restaurants in Rhode Island and South Coast Massachusetts pump out clam fritters (also called "clam cakes") by the dozens and even the hundreds every day, so it would be impractical for most eateries to start with a from-scratch batter. Many places turned years ago to using one of the good-quality commercial fritter mixes that are made and sold in the region. (See One Batter Mix, Three Ways, page 15.) But fritter batter is not all that easy to find in retail markets, so my friend Susan Maloney's aunt Phyllis Corcoran, from Fall River, Massachusetts, kindly shares her recipe for the fabulous fritters for which she's renowned.

1	egg
3	tablespoons vegetable oil
¾	cup clam juice (liquor drained from clams, bottled juice, or a combination)
¼	cup milk, whole or low-fat
1½	cups all-purpose flour
2	teaspoons baking powder
½	teaspoon salt, plus more if necessary
1	cup finely chopped drained hard-shell clams

Vegetable oil for frying

Malt or cider vinegar or lemon wedges

Bottled hot sauce

1. In a small bowl, whisk together the egg and oil. Whisk in the clam juice and milk.

2. Combine the flour, baking powder, and salt in a large bowl. Whisk in the egg mixture and stir in the clams. The batter should be the consistency of thick cake batter. Adjust by adding a little more flour or liquid as necessary.

3. In a large, deep frying pan, heat about 2 inches of oil to 370°F. Dip a teaspoon (see Note) in the oil to coat it, then spoon out one rounded spoonful of batter, slide it into the hot oil, and cook for 2 to 3 minutes, turning once with tongs, until puffed and golden. Drain on paper towels. Taste this first fritter for seasoning, adding more salt to the batter if necessary. Continue to fry the fritters, a few at a time, until all the batter is used.

4. Serve with vinegar or lemon wedges and hot sauce.

NOTE: Aunt Phyllis uses a long-handled iced tea spoon to scoop out the batter. It keeps her hands from coming too close to the hot oil and also creates a nicely shaped and sized fritter.

Makes about 3 dozen fritters

Block Island Gold Nuggets with Charlie Sauce

Block Island lies about 12 miles off the coast of the Rhode Island mainland. Swordfish is king on "the Block," where it has been hauled in by generations of fishermen from the deep Gulf Stream waters that run not far off the island. Always highly prized for its sweet, meaty flesh, these days swordfish is more scarce and pricier than ever — hence the designation of these crispy, succulent little nuggets as "Block Island gold." At Chopmist Charlie's in Jamestown, the appetizer is served with their famous Charlie Sauce — the perfect piquant dipping accompaniment.

Canola or peanut oil
    for frying

¾   cup all-purpose flour

½   teaspoon salt

¼   teaspoon freshly
     ground black pepper

¼   teaspoon Cajun
     seasoning blend

½   cup pancake mix,
     such as Bisquick

½   cup milk or water

1   cup panko crumbs
    (see Notes)

1   pound trimmed and
    skinned swordfish,
    cut in 1½-inch cubes

Lemon wedges

Charlie Sauce *(next page)*

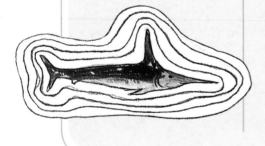

1. For the nuggets, heat the oil over medium heat in a deep fryer or a deep skillet until it reaches 350°F (see Notes).

2. In one bowl, stir together the flour, salt, pepper, and Cajun seasoning. In a second bowl, whisk together the pancake mix and milk until smooth. Place the crumbs in a third bowl. Dredge the swordfish in the flour and shake off the excess. Dip in the batter, let the excess drip off, and dredge in the crumbs.

3. Working with about one third of the fish at a time, slide the nuggets into the hot fat and fry until the crumbs are golden brown, 2 to 3 minutes. Drain on paper towels.

4. Serve with lemon wedges and the Charlie Sauce for dipping.

NOTES: Panko crumbs are crisp Japanese-style breadcrumbs. As a substitute, use fresh white bread crumbs; dry them out in a 200-degree oven for about 30 minutes until crisp, and measure after drying. (See Mail-Order Sources, page 240.)

   If making only half a recipe of nuggets, you can shallow-fry the fish in ½ to ¾ inch of oil (see Frying Basics, page 146).

4 servings

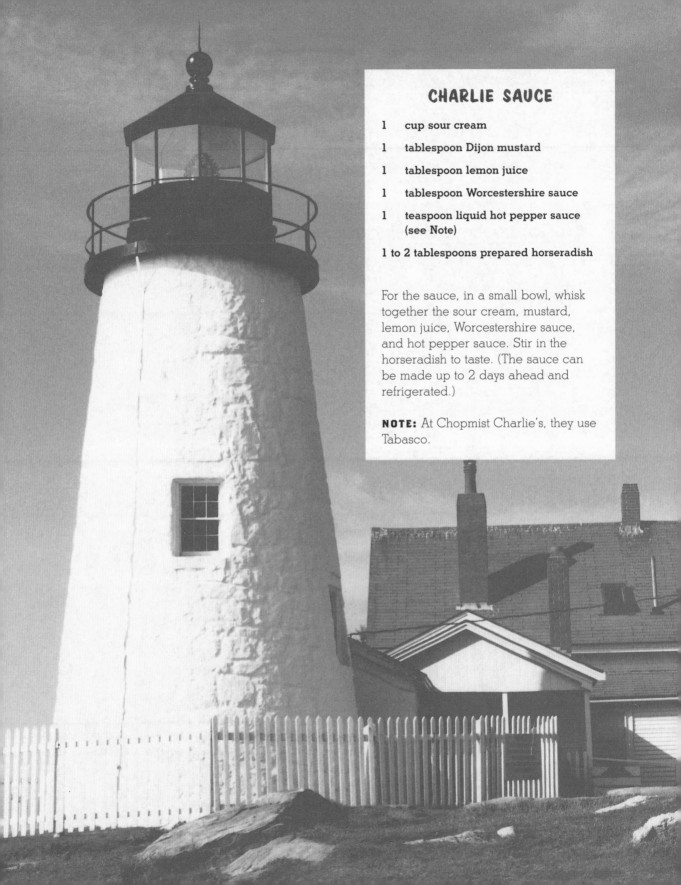

CHARLIE SAUCE

1   cup sour cream

1   tablespoon Dijon mustard

1   tablespoon lemon juice

1   tablespoon Worcestershire sauce

1   teaspoon liquid hot pepper sauce (see Note)

1 to 2 tablespoons prepared horseradish

For the sauce, in a small bowl, whisk together the sour cream, mustard, lemon juice, Worcestershire sauce, and hot pepper sauce. Stir in the horseradish to taste. (The sauce can be made up to 2 days ahead and refrigerated.)

NOTE: At Chopmist Charlie's, they use Tabasco.

Seahorse Tavern

Noank, Connecticut

This place has everything going for it — great food, including fabulous renditions of local specialties, friendly service, reasonable prices, a funky bar with fish scales painted on the ceiling, and a slightly dressier dining room suitable for more special occasions. The Seahorse has no water views, but it's located smack in the middle of a marina, so you feel intimately connected to the salty Noank harbor scene. (In addition, a local artist has painted a mural on the dining room wall depicting the water view that you'd see if only the room had windows!) The Seahorse has been in the village of Noank in one form or another for more than 50 years, but it was recently purchased and spruced up by Bob Sader, a well-respected chef in these parts. Locals hang out here, businessmen make a beeline for lunch, and tourists search it out.

Lots of people start with Seahorse's famous Clams Casino. Topped with chopped veggies and crispy bacon, a platter of these can easily make a lunch. Grilled mussels are another specialty. The Seahorse prides itself on Noank chowder, a "clear" chowder made with no milk or cream whatsoever, which is the style typical of this part of the Connecticut coast. In addition to heaping fisherman's platters of beer-battered fish, scallops, clams, shrimp, and fries, the menu also features a few Italian seafood specialties, including a fabulous Calamari Fra Diavolo and Shrimp Oreganata with Pomodoro and Feta. A tavern menu at the Seahorse offers lighter fare, such as soups, seafood rolls, and salads.

Rhode Island Stuffies

When Chuck Masso, owner of Chopmist Charlie's in Jamestown, Rhode Island, told me his stuffies (baked stuffed clams) had won first prize in the International Quahog Festival a few years ago, my ears pricked up. I had eaten a lot of bad stuffed clams by then — too bready, too gummy, underseasoned, and so on — so I came to his with a touch of cynicism. Well . . . the judges were correct, and Chuck has every right to be proud of this fabulous rendition of the Rhode Island classic. Chopmist Charlie's stuffies are of a heroic size — two could easily make a lunch — so if you like them a little daintier, just use smaller quahog shells.

3	tablespoons olive oil
1	cup (10 to 12 slices) finely minced bacon (pulse in food processor or chop fine until bacon is almost a paste)
8	garlic cloves, minced
1	cup finely chopped celery
1	cup finely chopped onion
2	quarts chopped hard-shell clams in juice (see Notes)
½	cup chopped parsley
¼	cup lemon juice
2	tablespoons liquid hot pepper sauce (see Notes)
2	tablespoons Worcestershire sauce
½	cup (1 stick) butter, cut in about 10 slices

Ingredients continue on next page

1. In a very large skillet or Dutch oven, heat the oil. Add the bacon, garlic, celery, and onion, and cook over medium heat, stirring frequently, until the bacon renders its fat and the vegetables soften, 10 to 15 minutes. Spoon off the excess fat, leaving about ¼ cup in the pan. Add the clams, parsley, lemon juice, hot pepper sauce, and Worcestershire sauce. Increase the heat to high and cook until bubbles begin to form around the edges and the mixture almost, but not quite, comes to a boil. Watch carefully: If the clams boil, they release too much liquid and become tough.

2. Reduce the heat to low. Add the butter and 6 cups of the crumbs. Cook over the gentle heat, stirring and adding enough more crumbs to absorb most of the liquid. The mixture should hold its shape when spooned out, but it should not be dry. Remove from the heat. Spoon the filling generously into the clamshells. (The clams can be prepared a day ahead and refrigerated or frozen.)

3. Preheat the oven to 425°F. Place the clams on a baking sheet and bake, uncovered, until the filling is heated through and lightly browned, about 25 minutes. Add about 10 minutes cooking time if the clams have been frozen. Run under a preheated broiler for a little additional browning, if you like.

Continued on next page

6 to 8 cups panko or other crisp dry bread crumbs (see Notes)

24 to 30 large (3- to 4-inch), clean quahog shells

Paprika

Lemon wedges

4. Sprinkle with paprika and serve with lemon wedges.

NOTES: You can buy clams in their juice from most fish markets. If the clams are in large pieces, lift them out of the juice and coarsely chop into ¼- to ½-inch chunks. The amount of juice varies, hence the range in the amount of breadcrumbs called for in the recipe.

At Chopmist Charlie's, they use Tabasco.

Panko crumbs are crisp Japanese-style bread crumbs. As a substitute, use fresh white bread crumbs; dry them out in a 200-degree oven for about 30 minutes until crisp, and measure after drying. (See Mail-Order Sources, page 240.)

Makes 2 to 2½ dozen large stuffed clams

ONE BATTER MIX, THREE WAYS

At the Seahorse Tavern in Noank, Connecticut, chef Bob Sader buys one premium breading mix and then uses it in various permutations, depending on what seafood he's frying. Before frying fish and shrimp, he dredges the seafood in the powdery breading mix and then dips it in a thick batter made by whisking beer and Old Bay seafood seasoning blend into the breading powder. His fish and shrimp emerge from the fryer enshrouded in a puffy crust, flavorful and golden brown. For fried clams and scallops, first he dips them in a thinner version of the same batter, then finishes them with a dusting of the powder, making for a lighter, crispier coating.

The Ultimate Stuffie

The Back Eddy Restaurant in Westport, Massachusetts, is a wonderful combination of upscale, down-to-earth, stylish, and unpretentious — and with fabulous food to boot. The menu is exciting, eclectic, and upbeat, featuring fresh takes on dishes from around the world as well as showcasing the best fresh ingredients from local farmers, fishermen, and purveyors. One of the chef's talents is taking traditional New England dishes — chowders, lobster dishes, Portuguese fish stews — and punching up their flavors and adding a modern tweak or two. Hence, I was not one bit surprised to encounter the best baked stuffed quahog I ever ate in my life at The Back Eddy. Chock-full of briny clams, Portuguese chourico, fresh herbs, and lots of garlic, this stuffie has the unexpected addition of cut-from-the-cob corn kernels, which create the perfect color contrast and burst of fresh flavor.

12 large quahogs, scrubbed

1 tablespoon olive oil

½ pound ground chourico (see Notes)

1 large onion, finely chopped

1 tablespoon chopped garlic

1 cup corn kernels (cut from 2 to 3 ears, or thawed frozen corn)

½ cup coarsely ground toasted Italian or Portuguese bread, plus additional if necessary (see Notes)

¼ cup chopped fresh oregano

Ingredients continue on next page

1. In a large pot, bring about 1 inch of water to a boil. Add the clams, return to the boil, reduce the heat to medium, and cook, covered, until the shells pop open, 5 to 10 minutes. Remove the clams with a slotted spoon and cool, reserving the cooking broth. Working over a bowl to catch and reserve the juices, scrape the clam meat out of the shells. Reserve 12 of the shells. Pulse the clam meat in a food processor until finely chopped.

2. In a large skillet, heat the oil. Add the chourico and onion and cook over medium heat, stirring frequently, until the meat is lightly browned, about 5 minutes. Add the chopped clams, garlic, and corn and cook for about 5 minutes. Add the reserved clam juices and 1 cup of the cooking broth, bring to a boil, and cook until the liquid is reduced by about half. Remove from the heat and stir in the breadcrumbs, oregano, and sage. If the mixture is dry, add a couple of tablespoons more of the reserved cooking broth. If too liquid, add a tablespoon or so more bread crumbs. Season to taste with salt and pepper.

Continued on next page

½ cup chopped fresh
sage

**Salt and freshly cracked
black pepper**

3 to 4 tablespoons butter

Lemon wedges

3. Loosely pack the stuffing into the reserved shells (can be made up to a day ahead and refrigerated).

4. Preheat the oven to 400°F. Arrange the stuffed clams on a baking sheet. Bake, uncovered, in the preheated oven until the tops are crusty and lightly browned, about 7 minutes. Place a slice of butter on top of each clam to melt, garnish with lemon wedges, and serve.

NOTES: The Back Eddy buys Mello brand chourico in bulk. If you can get only the sausage in its casing, peel off the casing and finely chop the meat in a food processor or with a large chef's knife.

For the breadcrumbs, The Back Eddy toasts sliced Portuguese bread in the oven until crisp and coarsely pulses it in the food processor.

4 servings

STUFFIES

Baked stuffed quahogs are affectionately known as "stuffies" around Narragansett Bay. A well-made stuffie is one of Rhode Island and southern Massachusetts' seminal contributions to American regional cuisine, but a good stuffie is labor intensive, and clams, which should be the primary ingredient, are getting quite pricey. As a result, many places cut corners by underseasoning and using too many breadcrumbs as filler, so you taste more starch than briny clam.

A good alternative to homemade stuffies are Whaler's Stuffed Quahogs (available in mild and spicy versions), a frozen product that has been made by a New Bedford, Massachusetts–based company for 35 years. In fact, many restaurants freely admit they've turned to buying these excellent stuffies, which are also available in some retail seafood markets in the region. The filling for Whaler's is a well-seasoned blend of breadcrumbs, chopped clams, onions, celery, green pepper, and linguiça.

Chopmist Charlie's

Jamestown, Rhode Island

From Chopmist Charlie's

BLOCK ISLAND GOLD NUGGETS WITH
CHARLIE SAUCE (PAGE 10)
RHODE ISLAND STUFFIES (PAGE 14)
ROASTED STRIPED BASS WITH
VEGETABLE GARNISH (PAGE 139)
GRANNY SMITH APPLE CRISP (PAGE 212)

Whatever the weather outside, when you walk into Chopmist Charlie's it feels like you've found a safe, secret haven. Two medium-sized rooms (bar on one side, dining room on the other), dark varnished wood, booths and tables, nautical decor with mounted fish hung on the wall . . . you get the picture. In fact, Jamestown, Rhode Island, a mile-wide island just over

the bridge from Newport, has itself been something of a well-kept secret that is fast being "discovered." Chuck Masso has owned Chopmist Charlie's for about 12 years and has created a year-round sanctuary for locals, tourists, and the yachtsmen who stroll up from one of the two large marinas on the island. He named his restaurant after the Chopmist Hill Inn, a legendary old place used for company outings in Scituate, Rhode Island, where the mist was so thick "you could chop it with a knife!"

Chuck loves New England food and believes in maintaining the simplicity and honesty of Yankee fare, but he is not averse to adding a few creative touches to his dishes. The seasoned flour for his Block Island swordfish nuggets, for instance, contains a touch of Cajun spice, and the fish is rolled in panko crumbs before frying. Chopmist's wonderful prizewinning Rhode Island Stuffies (baked stuffed clams) are chock-full of clams and enlivened with fresh parsley and a good shot of Tabasco sauce. Chuck often goes fishing himself on summer weekends; his father expertly fillets the catch, and much of it makes its way to Chopmist's kitchen. And the old-fashioned desserts — a very chocolatey cake, Grape-Nuts pudding, pies, and warm apple crisp — are homemade, comforting, and delicious.

Clams Casino

Chef Bob Sader of the Seahorse Tavern in the tiny coastal Connecticut town of Noank uses an interesting technique to open the clams for his dazzling casino preparation. After getting the clam knife between the two shells, he slices right through the clam, longitudinally, so that each bite of clam is half as big and already tenderized — less chewy. If you don't think you can master this technique, ask your fish store manager to do it for you. The Seahorse's appetizer portion of Clams Casino is huge (you can make a main course out of it), so I've cut down the recipe for making these at home.

12   half-dollar-sized hard-shell clams

¼   cup Seahorse Tavern Garlic-Lemon Butter (see page 25)

½   cup crisp dry bread crumbs, such as panko crumbs (see Note)

¼   cup coarsely chopped red bell pepper

2   tablespoons parsley sprigs

½   teaspoon paprika

½   teaspoon salt

½   teaspoon freshly ground black pepper

2   slices bacon, cut in 24 pieces

Lemon wedges

1. Open the clams by cutting through the shell and then slicing through the clam muscle itself longitudinally. Loosen the muscle where it attaches to the shell, leaving as much juice as possible in the clam. (See How to Shuck Clams, page 34). Divide the clam halves among four individual gratin dishes or place on a baking sheet. Preheat the oven to 450°F.

2. Place about 1 teaspoon of Garlic-Lemon Butter on each clam. To make the crumbs, combine the breadcrumbs, bell pepper, parsley, paprika, salt, and pepper in a food processor. Pulse to grind the mixture to a fine texture. Spoon about ½ tablespoon of the crumb mixture over each clam. Top with a bacon piece.

3. Place in the preheated oven and bake until the bacon browns and the butter is bubbly, about 10 minutes. If the bacon is not crisp enough, put the clams under the broiler for a minute or so. Garnish with lemon wedges before serving.

NOTE: Panko crumbs are crisp Japanese bread crumbs. Look for them in the Asian section of the supermarket. As a substitute, use fresh white bread crumbs; dry them out in a 200-degree oven for about 30 minutes until crisp, and measure after drying. (See Mail-Order Sources, page 240.)

4 servings, 6 half-clams each

Essex Steamers

Woodman's steamers are the real deal — hefty clams, expertly steamed, popping out of their shells, and served up, unapologetically, with only their steel-gray broth and some melted butter for dunking. They are plainspoken Yankee goodness in a (huge) bowl. Like his grandfather and namesake, Larry Woodman believes steamers should be large (fuller flavor, he explains), so he requests 2½- to 3-inch clams. The bellies firm up nicely as they cook.

1   **tablespoon cornmeal**

6   **pounds steamer clams**

½   **cup (1 stick) butter, melted**

1. Fill a large bowl or pot half full of cold water. Add the cornmeal. Scrub the clams if they are muddy and then soak in the cold water for at least 2 hours, changing the water a couple of times. Drain and rinse well again.

2. Add ½ inch of water in the bottom of one or two large pots. Put the clams in the pot, cover, and turn the heat to high. When the water begins to bubble up, reduce the heat and uncover. Return the heat to high and cook uncovered until the bubbles come up again. Repeat alternating low and high heat about four more times, until the shells are completely open and the bellies look firm, a total of about 10 minutes. The clams should come out of their shells easily.

3. Use a slotted spoon to transfer the clams to a serving bowl. Pour the cooking liquid into a couple of glass measuring cups and let the grit settle to the bottom. Pour off the clear gray broth into serving cups. Pour the melted butter into another set of serving cups.

4. To eat, pull the black skin off the edge and neck of the clam. Hold the clam by its neck and dunk first into broth to rinse, then into the melted butter.

4 to 6 appetizer servings

Evelyn's Clam Cakes

If you order clam cakes in Rhode Island or South Coast Massachusetts, don't expect anything at all like a delicate, lightly bound crab cake. Clam cakes (often called clam fritters) are hefty, deep-fried dollops of baking powder batter embedded with chopped clams. At their worst, when they're leaden and greasy with scarcely a trace of clam, they are the butt of jokes and are nicknamed "sinkers." At their best, clam cakes are light and crispy, with a clean clam tang — and some of these can be had at Evelyn's Drive-In in Tiverton. Serve them with a cruet of vinegar for sprinkling, another Rhode Island habit. Evelyn's recipe calls for using a fritter mix. For a homemade version, follow the recipe for Aunt Phyllis's Fabulous Famous Clam Fritters, page 9.

Canola oil for frying

2   cups clam cake or fritter mix (see Notes)

½   cup chopped sea clams, drained of most of their juice

½   cup bottled clam juice or juice from the chopped clams, or a mixture (see Notes)

¼ to ½ cup warm water, plus additional if necessary

Malt or cider vinegar

1. Heat the oil over medium heat in a deep fryer or deep pot until it reaches 300°F. (See Notes.)

2. In a large bowl, combine the clam cake mix and clams. Add the clam juice and begin to stir with a wooden spoon. It will be very dry at this point. Start adding the warm water by stirring it in gently but thoroughly; gradually add water until the batter reaches the consistency of peanut butter. Do not overmix.

3. Using a 1-ounce scoop or a tablespoon, drop the batter by spoonfuls into the hot fat. Do not crowd the pan. Fry slowly, turning once or twice, until the clam cakes are golden and cooked through, 4 to 5 minutes. Drain on paper towels. Repeat the process with the remaining batter. (Cooked clam cakes can be kept warm in a very low oven for a few minutes.)

4. Serve with vinegar for sprinkling.

Continued on next page

NOTES: Evelyn's uses Drum Rock clam fritter mix (see Mail-Order Sources, page 240). The listed ingredients are flour, whey, baking powder, and salt.

Chopped hard-shell clams often come packed in copious clam juice. You can use this juice in place of bottled clam juice.

If the low frying temperature doesn't work well for you at home, try increasing to 325°F or 350°F.

Makes about 3 dozen

HOW TO CLEAN CLAMS

These days, most hard-shell clams arrive at the market in a fairly clean state. Usually all they need is to be soaked in cold water for about an hour and given a quick scrub with a stiff brush before cooking.

Soft-shell (steamer) clams need more attention, whether you purchase from a fish market or dig them yourself.

1. First, rinse the clams well and scrub them with a stiff brush.

2. Let the clams soak in a large bowl or pot of cold water, along with a tablespoon or so of cornmeal or flour, which helps the creatures disgorge any internal mud. About an hour should do it for relatively clean clams, but if they're very muddy, let them stand for a couple of hours, changing the water a few times.

3. Finish with a final scrub and rinse. Discard any clams that are not tightly closed. To ensure a mud-free mouthful, many people dunk each steamer in the clam broth to rinse it again before popping it into their mouths.

"Grilled" Mussels

They've always been on the menu at the Seahorse Tavern in Noank, Connecticut, they've always been called "grilled" even though they're roasted, and they've always been a hit. These mussels are perfect make-ahead hors d'oeuvres for parties. Just pop an already-prepared batch in the oven, and they're ready to serve in just a few minutes!

32   **medium-sized mussels (about 1½ pounds), scrubbed**

½   **cup dry white wine**

About ¼ cup Garlic-Lemon Butter (next page), softened

½   **cup crunchy bread crumbs, such as panko crumbs (see Note)**

Parsley sprigs

Lemon wedges

1. Place the mussels and wine in a large kettle and bring to a boil over high heat. Stir, cover, reduce the heat to medium-high, and cook just until the mussels begin to open, 4 to 8 minutes. Drain and discard mussels that did not open. Break each mussel shell at the hinge; discard half of the shell, leaving 32 mussels nestled in a half shell. Arrange the mussels on a baking sheet.

2. Place about ½ teaspoon of the garlic butter on each mussel and sprinkle lightly with the crumbs. (The mussels can be prepared ahead to this point. Wrap well with plastic wrap and refrigerate for up to 1 day or freeze.)

3. Preheat the oven to 450°F. Place the baking sheet in the oven; roast until the bread crumbs are golden brown and the butter is bubbly, about 10 minutes. Garnish with parsley and lemon wedges before serving.

NOTE: Panko crumbs are crisp Japanese bread crumbs. Look for them in the Asian section of the supermarket. As a substitute, use fresh white bread crumbs; dry them out in a 200-degree oven for about 30 minutes until crisp, and measure after drying. (See Mail-Order Sources, page 240.)

4 servings

Garlic-Lemon Butter

This lovely parsley-flecked garlic and lemon butter is always on hand at the Seahorse Tavern in Noank, Connecticut. They use it in several of their most popular dishes, including Clams Casino (page 20), and "Grilled" Mussels (preceding page). It's also wonderful melted over grilled fish, chicken, meat, or steamed vegetables — in short, use it with abandon on most everything except dessert!

½ **cup (1 stick) butter, softened**

1 **tablespoon chopped garlic**

1 **tablespoon finely chopped parsley**

¼ **teaspoon salt**

⅛ **teaspoon freshly ground black pepper**

2 **tablespoons lemon juice**

1 **tablespoon dry white wine**

1. Combine all the ingredients in a mixing bowl. Use an electric mixer to beat together, or combine well by hand using a large fork.

2. Set aside for at least 30 minutes to allow flavors to blend before using. (The butter can be stored in a covered container in the refrigerator for several days, or frozen.)

Makes ½ cup

Evelyn's Drive-In

Tiverton, Rhode Island

From Evelyn's

CLAM CAKES (PAGE 22)
PAN-GRILLED SEA SCALLOPS (PAGE 111)
GRAPE-NUTS PUDDING (PAGE 211)

When Domenic and Jane Bitto bought Evelyn's from the original owner about 20 years ago, they decided to keep the same old-fashioned look and comfy feel of the place (and the original sign in the crushed seashell parking lot), while at the same time modernizing the kitchen and making other subtle updates. Evelyn's is a good deal more than a drive-in. Yes, you can still go to the window and order takeout to eat at one of their picnic tables perched on Nannaquaket Pond, an inlet of the lovely Sakonnet River. But you can also relax on their outdoor patio, or indoors in the cozy dining room, and receive waitress service.

The menu at Evelyn's is broad. Fried seafood is superb — whole-belly clams, sweet scallops, shrimp baskets, all lightly breaded and cooked in clean oil. Evelyn's deep-fried clam cakes, those Rhode Island fritters that are only occasionally (in my opinion) worth the calories, are light and crispy — some of the best I'd ever eaten. The center cut of deep-fried cod is so large that it covers the whole plate, and Dom's simple grilled scallops are better than those in many a fancier, pricier establishment. For non-fish people, there's meatloaf, baked ham, grilled chicken, and chicken and meat pies, as well as a couple of other local curiosities — chow mein sandwiches and coffee milk (see Rhode Island's Quirky Cuisine, page 188). Evelyn's sweetly spiced Grape-Nuts Pudding, made by Jane Bitto, is as good an old-fashioned dessert as you can get in New England.

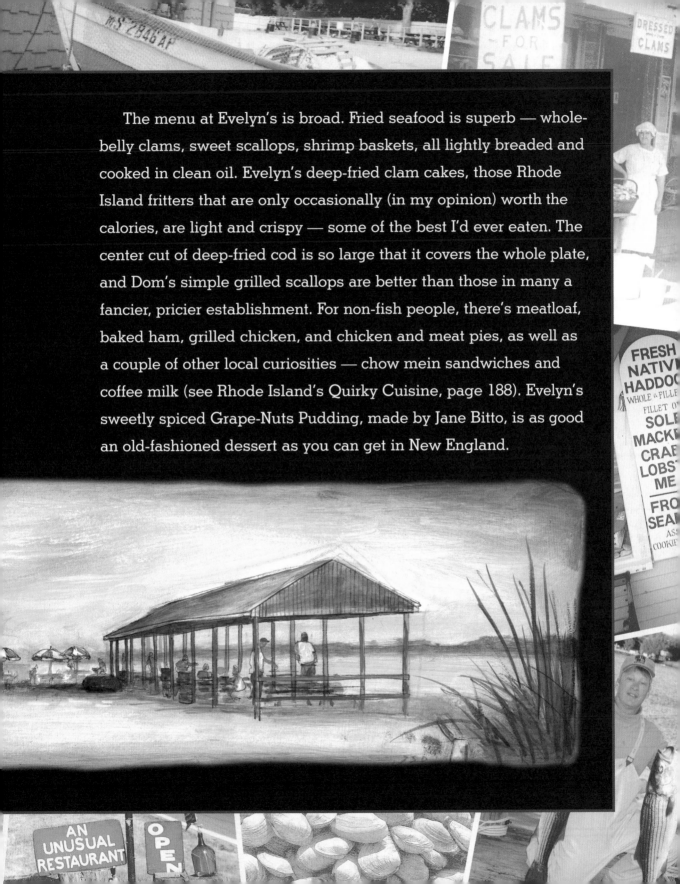

Oysters Mornay

These oysters are one of the most popular appetizers at J's Oyster Bar in Portland, Maine — and no wonder, for this marriage of briny oysters cloaked with a cheese-rich, sherry-laced Mornay sauce has to be divinely inspired. The oysters roast briefly in a hot oven until just barely cooked and are then finished under the broiler, so that the sauce is bubbly and flecked with brown. To open the oysters, see How to Shuck Oysters on page 109, or ask the fish market to perform the chore.

1   cup shredded Swiss cheese

⅓   cup dry sherry

1   tablespoon chopped parsley

1   tablespoon butter, softened

1   tablespoon flour

1   cup half-and-half

¾   teaspoon salt

½   teaspoon freshly ground black pepper

24   raw oysters on the half shell

Parsley sprigs for garnish

1. To make the Mornay sauce, combine the cheese and sherry in a medium saucepan. Place over medium-low heat and cook, whisking almost constantly, until the cheese melts. (The mixture will smooth out as the cheese melts.) Stir in the parsley.

2. Meanwhile, work the butter and flour together with a fork or your fingers to make a cohesive paste. Add the butter–flour mixture to the cheese mixture a few small chunks at a time. Cook over medium heat, whisking until the mixture is thick and bubbly. Whisk in the half-and-half, bring to a boil, and reduce heat to medium. Cook, whisking constantly, until the sauce is smooth, thickened, and reduced, about 5 minutes. Season with salt and pepper to taste. (The sauce can be made up to a day ahead and refrigerated.)

3. Preheat the oven to 375°F. Arrange the oysters on a baking sheet and spoon a scant tablespoon of sauce over each oyster. Roast in the preheated oven until the sauce is bubbly, 8 to 10 minutes.

4. Finish the oysters by placing them close to the element under a preheated broiler until the sauce is flecked dark brown, about 1 minute.

5. Garnish with parsley and serve.

4 servings (6 oysters each)

Wellfleet Oysters on the Half Shell

Oysters are named after the bay they're harvested from, and Cape Cod Wellfleets (from that town's nutrient-rich tidal bay) are some of the most prized in the world. When these local oysters are plentiful, especially in the winter months, Land Ho! in Orleans promptly puts them up on their menu board as a special, and happy customers slurp them up by the dozens and dozens. A squirt of lemon or a dollop of this simple cocktail sauce is the only embellishment they require.

Land Ho! Cocktail Sauce

1   cup chili sauce

¼   cup ketchup

3   generous tablespoons prepared horseradish

1   tablespoon fresh lemon juice

Pinch of onion powder

Freshly ground black pepper

Oysters

24 chilled Wellfleet or other good oysters (see Note)

Green leaf lettuce

Lemon wedges

1. For the cocktail sauce, in a medium bowl, whisk together the chili sauce, ketchup, horseradish, lemon juice, and onion powder. Season with pepper to taste.

2. Refrigerate the sauce for at least 1 hour to blend flavors. May be stored for up to 3 days.

3. Shuck the oysters (or have them shucked at the fish market) and cut them away from the muscle.

4. Arrange lettuce leaves over a bed of crushed ice. Arrange oysters on the lettuce. Garnish with the lemon wedges and serve with the cocktail sauce.

NOTE: The U.S. Food and Drug Administration warns that people with immune disorders and some other conditions should avoid eating raw seafood because it may pose serious health risks.

4 servings

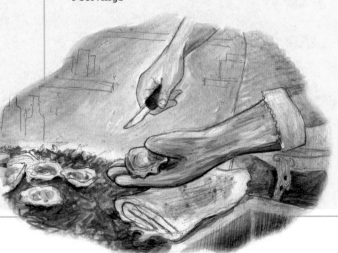

Crab Louis Spread

Mike and Libby Radcliffe wanted a simple appetizer to add to their menu at Thurston's Lobster Pound in Bernard, Maine — one that would showcase another of Maine's native shellfish — so they adapted this "crab Louis" spread from an old James Beard cookbook, adding even more of the sweet local crabmeat than the original recipe called for. It's just the right light nibble to help while away the time as you wait for your shore dinner to cook.

½   **cup mayonnaise**

2   **tablespoons bottled chili sauce**

1   **tablespoon grated onion**

1   **tablespoon chopped parsley**

Few grains cayenne pepper

½   **pound fresh crabmeat**

1 to 2 tablespoons heavy cream

Good-quality crackers

1. In a medium mixing bowl, stir together the mayonnaise, chili sauce, onion, parsley, and cayenne. Add the crabmeat and 1 tablespoon of the cream and fold the mixture together, taking care not to mash up the crab too finely. If the mixture is not quite thin enough to spread, add the remaining tablespoon of cream. Refrigerate for at least 2 hours to allow flavors to blend.

2. Serve surrounded by crackers. Spread the crab mixture on the crackers.

4 to 6 servings

Hot Crab Dip

At Tidal Falls Lobster Restaurant in Hancock, Maine, this sweet hot crab appetizer is presented in small individual ramekins, enough for one or two servings. This recipe translates beautifully to home cooking and entertaining, because it's even better if made at least a few hours ahead so that the flavors have a chance to meld and intensify.

1   (6-ounce) package cream cheese, softened

1   cup fresh lump-style crabmeat, picked over

1   tablespoon fresh lemon juice

2   teaspoons minced onion

Salt and freshly ground black pepper

Crackers or fresh raw vegetables, or both

1. In a mixing bowl, combine the cream cheese, crabmeat, lemon juice, and onion. Mix with a large fork to combine well. Season with salt and pepper to taste. Transfer to a 2- to 3-cup ramekin, smoothing the top. (This recipe can be made ahead and refrigerated for up to 2 days.)

2. Preheat the oven to 350°F. Bake the crab dip until pale golden brown on top and heated through, 25 to 35 minutes.

3. Serve hot or warm. Spread on crackers, or use raw vegetables for dipping.

4 to 6 servings

COOKING WITH YOUR EARS

When things get busy at Two Lights Lobster Shack in Cape Elizabeth, Maine, owner Martha Porch can tell her cooks at the fryers when the fried shrimp, clams, and other seafood is done by listening for the change of pitch as the food fries. "When the food first goes into the oil, there's a hissing and a bubbling sound," she says. "Then, when I hear a lighter, less bubbly pitch, I can call across the room and tell them it's time to pull it out."

Tidal Falls Lobster Restaurant

Hancock, Maine

Is it a lobster pound or is it a nature preserve? Actually, Tidal Falls Lobster Restaurant is both. The scenic property surrounding the restaurant was acquired a few years ago by a nature conservancy, but the group continues to run the restaurant as a way to generate income for the organization. Tidal Falls had been a popular local eatery (and something of a well-kept secret from tourists) for decades, and it's not surprising that the nature folks coveted the property, for this is a particularly beautiful and serene spot in a state

loaded with scenic beauty. As you sit at a picnic table right at the very edge of the shore, enjoying a sweet crabmeat roll or cracking open a seawater-steamed, locally caught lobster, you can watch the dramatic white water of a reversing falls and catch glimpses of native wildlife, including seals, ospreys, and the occasional eagle.

All the food on Tidal Falls' simple menu is excellent. Owned and operated for more than 40 years by two brothers, one of whom married a French woman, many of the dishes here still evince a decidedly Gallic flair. Everything at Tidal Falls is home-made, and as many ingredients as possible are locally grown or caught. Their Fresh-Squeezed Lemonade (made with bits of lemon peel), delectable Hot Crab Dip appetizer (made with local crab), succulent, Garlicky Mussels, fried fresh seafood, and rich, buttery Blueberry-Raspberry Dessert Squares — and everything in between — are honest Down East fare, but with a slightly sophisticated twist. The conservancy encourages visitors to patronize the restaurant or bring their own picnic and enjoy this magical little park.

HOW TO SHUCK CLAMS

• **To shuck hard-shell clams** that are to be eaten raw, use a clam knife, which has a squat, wide blade and a thick handle for easy gripping. To protect your hand, hold the clam with a folded cloth or oven mitt.

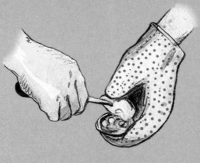

• **Insert the knife** between the two shells, opposite the hinge. Once the knife is in, if you want the clam to be intact, carefully work the knife along the top shell. (If you want to slice the clam in half longitud- inally, as for Seahorse Clams Casino [page 20], move the knife straight back through the clam meat to the hinge.)

• **Pry open the shell** and run the knife around the clam meat to free it, pre- serving as much of the clam juice as you can.

• **If you are using the hard-shell clams** in a cooked dish and do not mind a small loss of flavor, a much easier method for extracting clams from their shells is to steam them in about 1 inch of water in a large pot set over high heat just until their necks begin to open, about 5 minutes. Or, place the clams on a baking sheet and roast in a 375°F oven just until the shells begin to crack open, about 10 minutes. After opening, cut through the muscle that holds the shells together.

• **Raw soft-shell clams are a good** deal easier to open than hard-shell. Simply run a small sharp knife around the edge of the shell to open. Working over a bowl to catch the liquor, cut the meat from the bottom shell. Slit the skin of the neck, or siphon, and pull off the black skin. If the clams look muddy, dunk gently in cold salted water.

• **Again, for easier opening,** blanch the soft-shell clams in a large pot of boil- ing water just until the clams begin to open, about 2 minutes. Transfer with a slotted spoon to a bowl of ice water to cool, then pro- ceed with opening as above. This method has the advantage of mak- ing the black neck skin much easier to peel off.

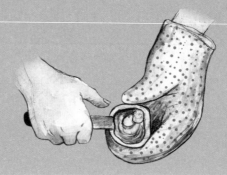

Roast Clams

These grilled clams, which are simplicity itself, were the first food I ever ate at The Place, in Guilford, Connecticut, and I was immediately hooked. They use a good-quality bottled cocktail sauce at The Place, but if you want to make your own, so much the better. You might try the Land Ho! Cocktail Sauce (page 29).

24   **littleneck clams**

⅓   **cup homemade or good-quality bottled cocktail sauce, plus additional, if desired**

4 to 5 tablespoons butter

Lemon wedges

1. Prepare a moderately hot hardwood or charcoal fire, or preheat a gas grill.

2. Place the unopened clams on the grill, cover, and cook just until the shells begin to pop open, 5 to 10 minutes. Pry off the top shells, daub the clams with cocktail sauce, and top each clam with a small piece (about ½ teaspoon) of butter.

3. Continue to cook on the grill until the clams are hot and the tops are lightly glazed with sauce and melted butter, about 5 minutes longer.

4. Serve with lemon wedges and a small bowl of cocktail sauce for dipping, if desired.

4 servings, 6 clams apiece

Littlenecks with Oil and Garlic

You can order the littlenecks in a zesty red sauce at Bristol, Rhode Island's Quito's, but I prefer this white sauce *(aglio e olio)* treatment. Provide plenty of good Italian bread for dunking in the copious juices, or serve it over freshly cooked thin-strand pasta.

4	tablespoons olive oil
5	garlic cloves, thinly sliced
32	littleneck clams, scrubbed
1	cup bottled clam juice or clam broth
1	tablespoon chopped fresh basil
½	teaspoon dried oregano
¼	teaspoon dried red pepper flakes
	Salt and freshly ground black pepper
2	tablespoons chopped flat-leaf parsley
	Italian bread (see Note)

1. In a large deep skillet or saucepan, heat the oil over medium heat. Add the garlic and cook just until the garlic turns pale golden, watching carefully so it doesn't burn, about 1 minute. Immediately add the clams, clam juice, basil, oregano, and dried red pepper flakes. Bring to a boil, reduce the heat, and simmer until the clam shells open, about 10 minutes.

2. Season the sauce with salt and pepper to taste. Transfer to a large bowl, sprinkle with parsley, and serve with Italian bread for sopping up the sauce (see Note).

NOTE: Or cook 12 ounces thin spaghetti until al dente and serve sauce over pasta.

3 to 4 first-course servings; 2 to 3 main-course servings

Fresh French-Fried Zucchini

Batter-dipping, crumbing, and deep-frying strips of zucchini is such a delicious concept that it's surprising that more places don't do something similar. Lenny & Joe's are crispy and golden brown — a heaping basket is the perfect starter to share for the table — and they're easy to re-create at home.

4   **medium-size zucchini (about 1½ pounds)**

1   **cup batter mix (see Note)**

1   **cup water**

2   **cups cracker meal (see Note)**

Vegetable oil for deep frying

Salt

1. Cut the zucchini into strips ¼- to ⅜-inch wide and about 2½ inches long. Pat dry on paper towels.

2. In a bowl, whisk the batter mix with the water to make a smooth batter. Place the cracker meal in another bowl.

3. In a large, deep frying pan heat about 2 inches of oil over medium heat to 350°F. (Or use a deep fryer if you prefer.)

4. Dip the zucchini into the batter, letting the excess drip off, and then dredge in the cracker meal. Transfer to a colander to gently shake off the excess meal. Slide into the hot oil and cook until nicely browned on all sides, 1 to 2 minutes. Remove with a slotted spoon, drain on paper towels, sprinkle with salt, and serve hot.

NOTE: Batter mix (see page 15) and cracker meal can be purchased in the breading section of the supermarket. If you can't find cracker meal, whir saltine crackers in a food processor until finely ground and smooth.

4 appetizer servings

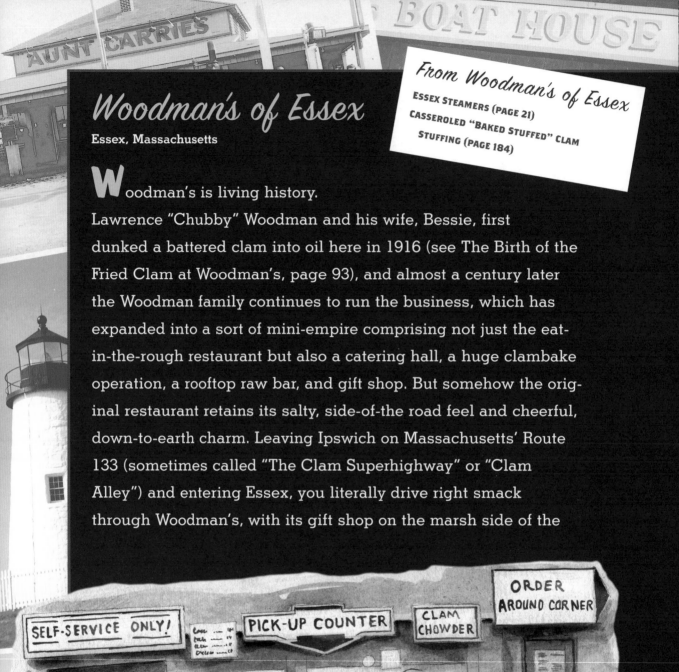

Woodman's of Essex

Essex, Massachusetts

From Woodman's of Essex

ESSEX STEAMERS (PAGE 21)
CASSEROLED "BAKED STUFFED" CLAM
STUFFING (PAGE 184)

Woodman's is living history.

Lawrence "Chubby" Woodman and his wife, Bessie, first dunked a battered clam into oil here in 1916 (see The Birth of the Fried Clam at Woodman's, page 93), and almost a century later the Woodman family continues to run the business, which has expanded into a sort of mini-empire comprising not just the eat-in-the-rough restaurant but also a catering hall, a huge clambake operation, a rooftop raw bar, and gift shop. But somehow the original restaurant retains its salty, side-of-the road feel and cheerful, down-to-earth charm. Leaving Ipswich on Massachusetts' Route 133 (sometimes called "The Clam Superhighway" or "Clam Alley") and entering Essex, you literally drive right smack through Woodman's, with its gift shop on the marsh side of the

road and the restaurant — where you can watch burly workers loading lobsters into outdoor cookers — on the other.

So, pull into the lot and join the line of eager, clam-hungry regulars and tourists, order at one window, pick up your tray at the other, and look for a seat at a wooden picnic table or old-fashioned booth where you join in the clatter and clamor and din that is an essential part of the Woodman's experience. Since, after all, we're at the source, I like to stick to the bivalve here. Order steamers — large, with often-broken shells and some grit, but full of sweet clam flavor — or a basket of the "original" whole-belly fried clams, made the same way they were a hundred years ago by first dipping in milk, then in a corn flour mixture and fried at a constant 350°F. They're the standard by which all others on the Clam Belt are judged. Round out the meal with a cup of chowder (unthickened and sweet), onion rings (slim and crispy), French fries, or creamy coleslaw. You'll leave happy and full — and be part of history.

Topside Seafood Sampler Platter

Okay, so if you can't import the fantastic view and convivial ambience of Flo's Topside Bar, you can certainly assemble all the right elements and re-create this raw bar at home. Since the small crabs native to New England don't contain much meat, Flo's buys sweet and meaty king crab legs from Alaska.

Seafood

A selection of all or some of the following:

Littlenecks on the half shell

Raw oysters on the half shell

Cooked shrimp in their shells (peel to eat)

Lobster claw and tail meat, cut in chunks

King crab legs

Condiments

Chili sauce

Horseradish

Lemon wedges

A selection of bottled hot sauces, which might include Tabasco (red and green), Frank's, and a couple of the super-hot Jamaican or other West Indian sauces

Oyster crackers for nibbling

1. Arrange the seafood on crushed ice on a large platter. Stick toothpicks in the lobster meat.

2. Provide small bowls so that guests can concoct their own sauces to taste.

Makes as many servings as your budget will allow.

Call

CHAPTER 3

Yankee Chowders, Seafood Stews, and Soups

As far as I'm concerned, bona fide homemade chowder or soup is the acid test of any eating establishment. Restaurants are ideally set up to make from-scratch soups — they have the requisite big pots, they have access to all the right fresh ingredients, and they can improvise a wonderful soup or stew from odds and ends of fish or vegetables that might otherwise be thrown away. So why oh why would any New England eatery worth its salt pork even *consider* resorting to "clam base" (a stale-tasting powdered seasoning additive) or to using a commercial frozen or canned product when all the right stuff is at their fingertips? The sad fact is that many do. However, there are enough reputable New England eateries making from-scratch chowders that thankfully one needn't totally despair. All the interesting regional chowder variations are represented in this chapter — clear and brothy, tomato-tinted, thick and rich, thin and milky — as well as some fabulous New England seafood stews. There's a recipe for the classic Maine lobster stew, which is simply a pristine brew of lobster chunks, rich milk, pooled melted butter, and a blushing sprinkle of paprika, and, the one nonseafood exception, that much loved New England specialty, a linguiça-laden Portuguese kale soup.

Lisa's Rhody Red Mixed Seafood Chowder

Lisa ("they call me Queen Quahog") Miller is the person in Flo's kitchen who builds this stand-out chowder. Lisa said, "You might even be tempted to call this a stew, we make it so thick with seafood. But we still call it a chowder, because, after all, it has the typical chowder elements of salt pork and potatoes." The addition of a bit (not much) of tomato purée at the end is what turns this chowder into a uniquely Rhode Island version of the brew. Serve with a basket of good chewy Italian or Portuguese bread.

1	cup diced salt pork (4 to 5 ounces)
1½	cups chopped bell peppers, preferably red, yellow, and orange
1	cup chopped onions
3	cups diced all-purpose potatoes (about 1 pound)
2	cups bottled clam juice
3	cups water
2	cups chopped hard-shell clams with any juice
¾	pound cod or scrod, cut in 1½-inch chunks
½	pound skinless salmon fillet cut in 1-inch chunks
½	pound shelled and deveined medium shrimp
½	pound bay scallops
½	pound crabmeat
1	cup tomato purée or canned tomato sauce

Salt and freshly ground black pepper

1. In a large soup pot, cook the salt pork over medium heat until the fat is rendered and the pork is crisp, about 15 minutes. Remove the pork bits with a slotted spoon, leaving the drippings in the pot.

2. Add the bell peppers and onions and cook over medium-high heat, stirring, for about 3 minutes. Add the potatoes, clam juice, and water, bring to a boil, reduce the heat, and simmer, covered, until the potatoes are tender, 10 to 15 minutes.

3. Add the clams with juice, cod, salmon, shrimp, scallops, crabmeat, and tomato purée. Bring to a boil, reduce the heat to medium-low, and simmer until the seafood is cooked through, about 5 minutes. Season with salt and pepper to taste. (If time allows, cool and refrigerate for 24 hours, which gives the chowder time to develop more flavor.)

4. Reheat gently and serve.

6 to 8 main-course servings

THE BEST CLAMS? DEPENDS ON WHO YOU ASK

There's a subtle but very definite variation in the taste of clams from one body of water to another. After 30 years of selling clams, **Eddie Martin,** of Gene's Seafood Market in Fairhaven, Massachusetts, insists he can tell where clams come from just from their taste — even after they've been smothered in breading and submerged in boiling oil.

Ginny Olsen, who comes from a fishing family that goes back several generations, now owns Oceanville Seafood in Deer Isle, Maine, and sells local clams to all the restaurants in the area, including Bagaduce Lunch in Penobscot (see page 192). "Maine clams are the best. Ours are harvested from the clean, cool waters around Stonington and Deer Isle, and they have a sweet, slightly salty flavor. Most are pulled by hand — without using a hoe — from the mud. The blackish shell tells you it's a mud clam. Mud clams are superior because they're much cleaner and have less grit than the lighter shelled sand clams."

Skip Atwood, who ran Ipswich's Clam Box for 10 years, says, "I could be blindfolded and open a can of clams and know where they're from. Clams from the Chesapeake are sweeter, and Maine's are more metallic."

Maureen Pothier, instructor at Johnson and Wales and lifelong Rhode Islander, says, "Obviously, the best clams come from Narragansett Bay."

"Call me biased, but I've never had another clam as good as the ones here in Wellfleet," says **Pat Woodbury,** a Cape Cod aquaculturalist.

"The Essex clam is the best in the world," says **Steve Woodman,** owner of Woodman's Restaurant in the Cape Ann town 40 miles northeast of Boston.

Noank Clear Clam Chowder

This clear chowder (broth only, no milk or cream) is typical of the style that has been cooked up for generations along a particular narrow stretch of New England coastline, from eastern Connecticut through western Rhode Island. The Seahorse Tavern in Noank, near Mystic, Connecticut, serves it proudly, almost as a badge of honor. Chef Bob Sader chops his own fresh quahogs, but if opening clams is not your special gift, you can buy chopped clams from a good fish market. Be sure to include the liquor they're packed in as part of the liquid in the chowder.

¾ cup finely diced salt pork (about 3 ounces)

1 large celery rib, chopped

1 large leek, white and pale green parts only, rinsed and chopped

1 medium onion, chopped

6 cups bottled or canned clam juice (or use the clam liquor as part of this quantity)

4 cups water

4 to 5 cups peeled and diced all-purpose potatoes (1½ pounds)

3 cups chopped hard-shell clams

2 teaspoons dried thyme, or 2 tablespoons chopped fresh

2 tablespoons chopped parsley

Salt and freshly ground black pepper

1. Cook the salt pork in a large soup pot over medium-low heat until the fat is rendered and the pork bits are crispy, about 15 minutes. Remove the pork with a slotted spoon and drain on paper towels, leaving the drippings in the pan.

2. Add the celery, leek, and onion to the pan drippings and cook, stirring frequently, until the vegetables begin to soften, about 6 minutes. Add the clam juice, water, potatoes, clams, and thyme. Bring to a boil, reduce the heat to medium-low, and cook, covered, until the potatoes are tender, about 15 minutes. Remove from the heat and let the chowder rest, partially covered, at cool room temperature for at least 1 hour, or refrigerate for up to 2 days.

3. Reheat gently. Adjust the liquid if necessary: Add more broth or water if too thick, or simmer for a few minutes to reduce if too thin. Stir in the parsley and season to taste with salt and pepper. Pass the crisp pork bits for sprinkling on top of the chowder, if desired.

8 first-course servings; 4 main-course servings

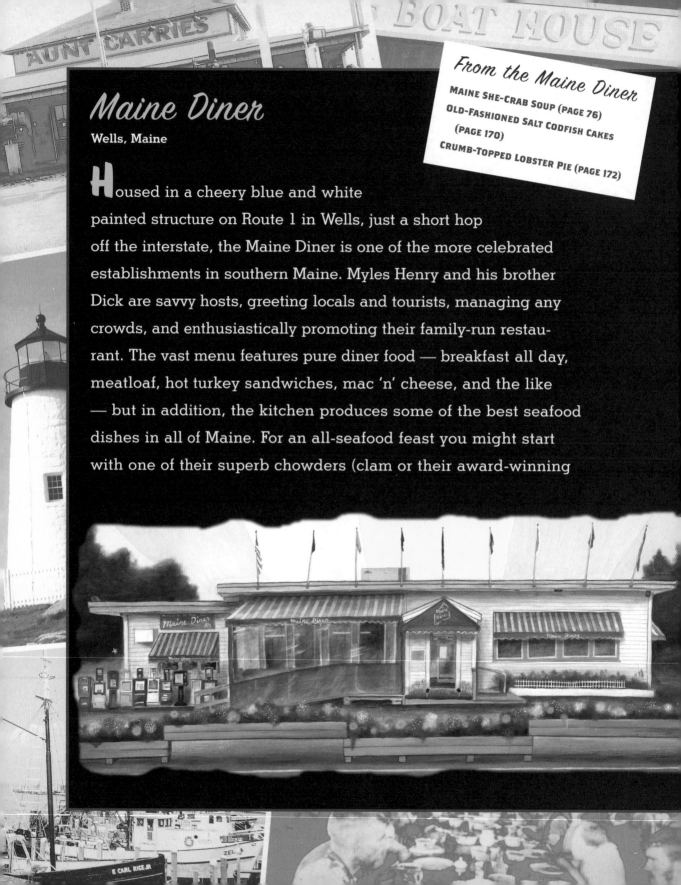

Maine Diner

Wells, Maine

From the Maine Diner

MAINE SHE-CRAB SOUP (PAGE 76)

OLD-FASHIONED SALT CODFISH CAKES (PAGE 170)

CRUMB-TOPPED LOBSTER PIE (PAGE 172)

Housed in a cheery blue and white painted structure on Route 1 in Wells, just a short hop off the interstate, the Maine Diner is one of the more celebrated establishments in southern Maine. Myles Henry and his brother Dick are savvy hosts, greeting locals and tourists, managing any crowds, and enthusiastically promoting their family-run restaurant. The vast menu features pure diner food — breakfast all day, meatloaf, hot turkey sandwiches, mac 'n' cheese, and the like — but in addition, the kitchen produces some of the best seafood dishes in all of Maine. For an all-seafood feast you might start with one of their superb chowders (clam or their award-winning

mixed seafood chowder) or
the creamy sherry-spiked
She-Crab Soup made
with local crabmeat.
Move on, perhaps, to a
small order of excellent
crumbed whole-belly fried
clams with a side of crisp
coleslaw, and then to a ramekin of
the Maine Diner's fabulous Crumb-Topped Lobster
Pie. Finish with a slice of home-baked pie-of-the-day (blueberry,
apple, or whatever fruit is in season), Grape-Nuts custard pudding, or a molasses-sweet Indian pudding topped with melting
vanilla ice cream.

The diner's other specialty is good old-fashioned — some
almost forgotten — New England dishes. Their codfish cakes,
made with salt cod and hand-mashed potatoes, are absolutely
scrumptious and are served with a side of soupy homemade
bacon-laced baked pea beans. Other Yankee specials include
New England Boiled Dinner, Red Flannel Hash, Salmon Pie,
and Yankee Pot Roast.

This place hums. Lines can be long, but while waiting you
can browse the cheerful gift shop and pick up a Maine Diner
t-shirt or a funny lobster claw visor as a souvenir.

CLAM CHOWDER WARS

The subject of how to make a proper Yankee clam chowder has provoked fierce disagreement for well over 150 years. Not only do people from different regions of New England (or even people from neighboring towns in the same region) argue about what constitutes an "authentic" chowder, but there is scarcely accord even as to which ingredients differentiate a chowder from other soups. Salt pork? (Not invariably.) Onions? (Almost always.) What kind of potatoes? (Adamant advocates for both boiling and russet.) Type of clams? (Usually chopped hard-shell — but not in Maine.) Broth, milk, cream, butter? (We find adherents to one or some or all of the above.) Herbs? (Usually none, but sometimes thyme.)

Regional distinctions tend to be slightly blurred now, but here are some of the traditional variations:

Southern New England clear chowder. Almost always starts with salt pork, thickened only with floury potatoes, and a broth-and-water base. Made with chopped hard-shell clams.

Boston- or New England–style chowder. A milk or cream base, flavored with salt pork, full of diced potatoes, and usually but not always thickened with a little (and sometimes with way too much) flour. Made with hard-shell clams.

Rhode Island red chowder. Like a typical clear, milk-free chowder, but with just enough tomatoes (usually puréed) to tint the broth a pretty reddish color. Sometimes made more like a chunky vegetable soup with clams, which most Yankees disdain as being too much like Manhattan chowder.

Milky Maine chowder. A milky, brothy base, not thickened with flour, usually (but not always) flavored with salt pork, and filled with cubed all-purpose Maine potatoes. Often uses soft-shell clams; when made with hard-shell, it's specified as "quahog chowder." Finished with pools of melted butter.

Nana's Haddock Chowder

This is my adaptation of the wonderful, simple New England haddock chowder served at J.T. Farnham's in Essex, Massachusetts. The "Nana" in the recipe title is owner Joe Cellucci's grandmother Lucy Davis, whose roots go way back on the North Shore and who was renowned for her chowder-making skills. The salt pork is essential in this recipe, as is, naturally, the freshest fish you can find.

¼ **pound salt pork, thinly sliced or diced**

½ **cup (1 stick) butter**

1½ **cups finely chopped onion**

3 **pounds haddock fillets**

4 **cups water**

8 **cups peeled and diced all-purpose potatoes (about 3 pounds)**

4 **cups whole milk**

Salt and freshly ground black pepper

1. In a large soup pot, cook the salt pork over medium-low heat, stirring occasionally, until the fat is rendered and the pork is crisp, about 15 minutes. Remove the salt pork pieces with a slotted spoon, leaving the drippings in the pan. Add the butter and melt over medium heat. Add the onions and cook, stirring frequently, for 5 minutes.

2. Meanwhile, trim the haddock by cutting off the thinner tail ends. Add the tail pieces to the pot and cook, turning once or twice, until the fish is cooked through, about 5 minutes. Add the remaining haddock to the pot, along with the water and potatoes. Bring to a boil, reduce the heat to medium-low, and simmer, covered, until the potatoes are tender and the fish is cooked through, about 15 minutes. As the haddock cooks, it will break up into smaller pieces. (The chowder base can be made a day ahead to this point and refrigerated.)

3. Reheat the chowder gently, add the milk, and simmer until heated through. Season to taste with salt and pepper.

16 first-course servings;
8 main-course servings

Portsmouth Seafood Chowder

Chef Jeff Graves at BG's Boat House in Portsmouth, New Hampshire, says that soups and chowders have a natural niche on most seafood restaurant menus — but especially in traditionally frugal New England, because chefs get to use up all those extra bits of fish that might not be suitable for an entrée. This deliciously rich chowder is BG's basic recipe, but Jeff sometimes makes substitutions depending on which seafood was freshest and most plentiful in the market that day.

2   **pounds haddock or other firm white fish**

¾   **pound sea scallops, chopped into rough ¾-inch dice**

2   **cups bottled or canned clam juice**

4   **cups water**

1½   **teaspoons Old Bay or other seafood seasoning blend**

2   **pounds all-purpose potatoes, peeled and diced (about 6 cups)**

¼   **pound bacon (4 to 5 slices), finely chopped**

1   **cup chopped onion**

2   **tablespoons cornstarch**

1   **cup half-and-half, plus additional if necessary**

Salt and freshly ground black pepper

1. Place the haddock and scallops in a large pot. Add the clam juice, water, and seafood seasoning. Bring to a boil. Reduce the heat to low and simmer until the seafood is almost but not quite cooked through, about 3 minutes. Remove the pan from the heat and set aside. Do not drain.

2. In a large saucepan, cook the potatoes in boiling salted water to cover until they are just tender, about 10 minutes. Drain and reserve the potatoes.

3. In a medium skillet, cook the bacon over medium heat until it is about half done, about 5 minutes. Add the onion and cook until the bacon is browned and the onions are softened, about 10 minutes longer.

Continued on next page

I Say Tomato, You Say Milk!

"THERE IS A WELL-WORN CONTROVERSY among chowder lovers as to which is correct, the kind made with milk or the kind made with tomato and water . . . Who knows? Furthermore, who cares? You should eat according to your own tastes as much as possible, and if you want to make a chowder with milk and tomato, crackers and potatoes, do it, if the result pleases you (which sounds somewhat doubtful, but possible)."

— M. F. K. Fisher

4. Using a slotted spoon, remove the seafood from its cooking liquid and transfer it to a bowl. Put the cornstarch in a small bowl and whisk in about ½ cup of the seafood poaching liquid until the mixture is smooth. Bring the seafood poaching liquid to a simmer and whisk in the cornstarch mixture. Bring to a boil, whisking constantly, and cook for about 2 minutes, until the base is smooth and thickened. Add the fish, scallops, potatoes, and bacon–onion mixture to the pot. Stir in the half-and-half, bring to a simmer, and season with salt and pepper to taste.

5. Refrigerate the chowder for at least 1 hour or for up to 2 days. Reheat gently, adjusting the seasonings and adding more liquid if necessary.

12 first-course servings; 6 main-course servings

Rhode Island Red Clam Chowder

Many Rhode Island restaurants, including Champlin's in Narragansett, list three kinds of chowder on their menus: clear, white, and red. Clear is brothy, white is milky (and sometimes flour-thickened), and red is usually clear, with some tomato and spice added. This recipe from Champlin's makes a pot of exemplary red chowder. At Champlin's, the cook makes the chowder with both sea clam strips (for flavor) and chopped quahogs, but at home, you can use whatever chopped hard-shell clams you can most easily obtain. Be sure to "cure" the chowder in the refrigerator for several hours, because this is when the good briny clam flavor really develops.

4   tablespoons butter

1   cup chopped onions

2   tablespoons Lawry's
     seasoned salt

6   cups chopped clams,
     plus their liquor

4   cups bottled or
     canned clam juice

6   cups water

6   cups peeled and
     diced all-purpose
     potatoes

½   cup condensed
     tomato soup

½   cup tomato purée
     or sauce

½   teaspoon cayenne
     pepper

Salt and freshly ground
     black pepper

1. In a large soup pot, melt the butter. Add the onions and seasoned salt, and cook over medium heat for 5 minutes. Add the clams and their liquor, the clam juice, and the water. Bring to a boil, reduce the heat to medium-low, and simmer, covered, for 30 minutes.

2. Add the potatoes. Bring to a boil, reduce the heat, and simmer until the potatoes are soft, about 15 minutes. Stir in the tomato soup, tomato purée, and cayenne, and simmer for 10 minutes. Cool the chowder and refrigerate for several hours or overnight.

3. Reheat gently. Adjust the seasonings and add more water if the chowder is too thick, and serve.

16 first-course servings;
8 main-course servings

Semi-Clear Clam Chowder

Oh, what a lovely chowder they "build" at Lenny & Joe's in Westbrook, Connecticut. It's done in typical southern New England style — untouched by flour, *mostly* clear broth, but with the addition of just enough evaporated milk to soften the rough edges of this primal brew. Try aging it for a day for even greater depth of flavor.

¾ cup chopped salt pork (about 3 ounces)

½ cup chopped onions

½ cup chopped celery

1 cup bottled clam juice, plus any liquor from clams

3 cups water

5 cups diced all-purpose potatoes (about 1½ pounds)

2 cups chopped hard-shell clams (see Note)

¼ cup evaporated milk

Salt and white pepper

1. In a large soup pot, cook the salt pork over medium-low heat, stirring occasionally, until the fat is rendered and the pork is crisp, about 15 minutes. Remove the pork bits with a slotted spoon, leaving the drippings in the pan.

2. Add the onions and celery to the pot and cook for 2 minutes. Add the clam juice and liquor, water, and potatoes, bring to a boil, reduce the heat, and cook, covered, until the potatoes are tender, about 15 minutes. Add the clams and simmer for 5 minutes. (Chowder may be prepared to this point and refrigerated for a day. Reheat gently before proceeding.)

3. Stir in the evaporated milk, season with salt and pepper to taste, and serve.

NOTE: Lenny and Joe use fresh quahogs (about 4 quarts) and shuck them at the restaurant. If you open your own, be sure to work over a bowl to save the precious, flavorful clam liquor. If there is any leftover chowder, reheat gently to avoid curding the milk.

6 to 8 first-course servings; 4 main-course servings

CLAM TYPING

There are two basic families of clams in New England: hard-shell and soft-shell. *HARD-SHELL CLAMS* are roundish, with a thick, almost rock-hard shell that remains tightly closed after they are taken from the salt water. They take skill to open by hand when raw, so when hard-shell clams are being used in cooking, some home cooks steam them or roast them on a baking sheet until they open slightly. *HARD-SHELLS* include the following types:

Sea clams, about 4 inches or more in diameter. They are too large to eat whole. The strip around the belly is referred to as a "clam strip" in the clam trade.

Quahogs (pronounced "co-hogs"), usually about 3 inches or more across; good when chopped for chowders or stuffing. (There is a bit of confusion here, because in some areas "quahog" is the generic name for hard-shell clams.)

Cherrystones, about 2½ inches across. They can be eaten raw on the half shell or used in cooking.

Littlenecks, youngest and smallest, less than 2 inches across. They are best for eating raw on the half shell or for Clams Casino (page 20).

SOFT-SHELL CLAMS are also known as **steamers.** Steamers have a shell that is a bit harder than an eggshell and a long fleshy black neck (siphon) that can protrude out of the shell. Steamers are easy to pry open by hand and a cinch to open after a quick blanching. Soft-shells come in a variety of sizes, from about 1½ to 3 inches across. The smaller size is preferable for most cooking uses, including steaming and deep-frying.

J's Oyster Bar

Portland, Maine

From J's

OYSTERS MORNAY (PAGE 28)
SEAFOOD BOUILLABAISSE ON
PASTA (PAGE 68)
SKILLET-FRIED HADDOCK (PAGE 151)

Two sisters own this friendly saloon-cum-restaurant, which is located right on the Portland waterfront. It's a bustling year-round hangout that is extremely popular with locals of all stripes but remains something of a well-kept secret from the tourists who clog the better-advertised eateries along busy Commercial Street. In summer, J's sets up a few tables outside (actually, at the edge of the parking lot), where you can sip a beer and throw your clamshells in the water while taking in the goings-on in the active Portland harbor. Inside, it's all cozy varnished wood booths looking out onto the bay, and a wraparound drinking bar.

J's is justly famous for its oysters and other raw bar specialties (served with a fabulous cocktail sauce that comes with a big chunk of fresh horseradish for personalizing your degree of heat). And oyster-lovers take note: During February, oysters are *free* here. There's no deep-fried food, but otherwise J's

menu covers the full range of New England seafood favorites. You can start with an outstanding Combination Cocktail, consisting of snowy fresh crabmeat, lobster chunks, raw scallops, shrimp, and oysters presented on a glistening bed of crushed ice. Oysters Mornay, with a Swiss cheese–rich topping, are one of the chef's favorites, as is the glorious Seafood Bouillabaisse. You can get an excellent cup of chowder or seafood stew or a piece of crumb-crusted, Skillet-Fried Haddock, or tie on a bib and plunge into J's dazzling New England shore dinner (chowder, steamers, lobster, and corn on the cob).

Creamy Cape Cod Clam Chowder

At Land Ho! in Orleans, on Cape Cod, they brew up enormous vats of their famed clam chowder — upward of 450 servings at a time — but the chef generously shared a drastically scaled-down recipe so that something akin to their chowder can be re-created at home. The chowder is a classic in the mid–New England (especially around the Cape and Boston) style — creamy, lightly flour-thickened, and full of briny chopped hard-shell clams.

5   tablespoons butter

1   large onion, chopped

¼   cup all-purpose flour

3   cups whole milk

2   cups bottled clam juice, or a combination of clam liquor and clam juice

2   cups water

5   cups diced all-purpose potatoes (1½ pounds)

2½ cups chopped sea clams or quahogs

¼   teaspoon celery salt

⅛   teaspoon celery seed

⅛   teaspoon garlic powder

1½ to 2 cups heavy cream

Salt and white pepper

1. In a large soup pot, melt the butter. Cook the onions over medium heat until softened, about 6 minutes. Sprinkle on the flour and cook, stirring, for 2 minutes. Add the milk, clam juice, and water, whisking until smooth. Add the potatoes, clams, celery salt and seed, and garlic powder and simmer until the potatoes are tender, about 15 minutes. Stir in enough cream to make a thick (but not too thick) and creamy chowder. Season with salt and pepper to taste.

2. Set aside at cool room temperature for at least an hour before serving or refrigerate for up to 2 days. Reheat gently.

8 to 10 first-course servings; 4 to 6 main-course servings

Milky Maine Steamer Chowder

Although Shaw's in New Harbor, Maine, respectfully declined to furnish their actual recipe, I have eaten their wonderful chowder enough times to be quite confident in re-creating a comparable version. This is a chowder in the quintessential Maine style — brothy, milky, and buttery, flavored with the subtle sea flavor of soft-shell steamer clams and their delicious broth, and thickened with only the starch in the potatoes. To maximize that good clam flavor, be sure to let this chowder "ripen" overnight.

2½ **pounds soft-shell clams, preferably small size**

6 **tablespoons butter**

1 **large onion, chopped**

3 **cups peeled and diced russet or all-purpose potatoes (about 1 pound)**

2 **cups clam broth or bottled clam juice or a combination of both**

2 **cups heavy or whipping cream**

Salt and freshly ground black pepper

Oyster crackers

1. Scrub the clams well and let them sit in a pot of cold water for at least an hour. Put the clams in a large pot, add about ½ cup water, cover, and bring to a boil. Reduce the heat to medium-low and steam until the clams open, 5 to 8 minutes. When cool enough to handle, remove the clams from their shells, working over the cooking pot to catch the juices. Pull the black skin off the necks. Strain the broth through cheesecloth or a clean linen towel and use it to make up all or some of the 2 cups clam liquid called for in the recipe.

2. Heat the butter in a large pot. Add the onion and cook over medium heat, stirring frequently, until softened, 5 to 8 minutes. Add the potatoes, clam broth, and cream, bring to a boil, reduce the heat to medium-low, and cook, covered, until the potatoes are tender, 10 to 15 minutes. Add the cooked clams along with any of their accumulated juices, and season to taste with salt and pepper.

3. Refrigerate the chowder uncovered until cold. Cover and refrigerate overnight or for up to 36 hours. Reheat gently, adding water and adjusting the seasoning as necessary. Serve with the oyster crackers on the side.

4 to 6 first-course servings; 2 to 3 main-course servings

Mussel Chowder

Thurston's Lobster Pound in Bernard, Maine, makes a different chowder every day. My favorite is the mussel chowder, which the Radcliffes, owners of Thurston's, adapted from a recipe on Epicurious.com. It's a light, delicate, creamy chowder, made pretty with finely diced carrots and orange bell peppers in addition to potatoes. One or two mussels in the shell go into each serving, where their glistening black shells create another dramatic color contrast. And it goes without saying that Thurston's uses only clean, locally caught wild mussels.

2   **cups water**

1   **cup bottled clam juice**

4   **pounds mussels, scrubbed**

6   **tablespoons butter**

3   **tablespoons olive oil**

4   **cups finely diced peeled potatoes**

1   **teaspoon salt, plus additional**

½   **teaspoon freshly ground black pepper, plus additional**

2   **carrots, peeled and finely diced**

2   **small leeks, cleaned well, white and pale green parts thinly sliced**

1   **yellow bell pepper, finely diced**

1   **large shallot, finely chopped**

3   **tablespoons minced garlic**

¾   **cup dry white wine**

1   **cup heavy cream**

1. In a large pot, bring the water and clam juice to a boil. Add the mussels and return to a boil. Reduce the heat to medium, and cook, covered, until the shells open, 4 to 8 minutes, depending on their size.

2. Using a slotted spoon, transfer the mussels to a bowl, discarding any that do not open. Set aside 16 mussels in their shells and shuck the rest. Pour the mussel broth into a glass measuring cup and let the sediment settle to the bottom.

3. In a large pot, heat the butter and oil. Add the potatoes, salt, and pepper. Cook over medium heat, stirring occasionally, for 5 minutes. Add the carrots, leeks, bell pepper, and shallot. Cook, covered, until the vegetables are tender, about 10 minutes. Add the garlic and cook, stirring, for 1 minute. Add the clean mussel broth (leaving any grit behind in the bottom of the measuring cup) and the wine, and simmer for 10 minutes. Add the shucked mussels and the cream and simmer for 5 minutes. Add the reserved mussels in their shells. Taste and season with additional salt and pepper if necessary. (The chowder is best when made ahead and refrigerated overnight.)

4. Reheat gently. Ladle into cups or bowls, making sure each portion contains at least one of the mussels in the shell.

16 first-course servings; 8 main-course servings

Mediterranean Seafood Stew

Its origins might be Mediterranean, but the use of super-fresh locally caught Maine seafood turns this stew into a spectacular New England dish, one of the most popular at Cod End Cookhouse in Tenants Harbor, Maine. When owner Anne Miller makes this at home, she adds a cup or two of white wine in place of the some of the water (and you could, too), but at the restaurant, it's wine-free. Either way, this stew is delicious and beautiful to look at — especially welcome on a chilly day.

¾   **cup good-quality olive oil**

3   **cups chopped leeks, white and pale green parts only**

3   **garlic cloves, finely chopped**

3   **cups chopped green bell pepper**

3   **cups thinly sliced celery**

1   **tablespoon fennel seed**

2   **teaspoons dried red pepper flakes**

2   **teaspoons turmeric**

1½   **teaspoons dried thyme**

2   **large cans (28 ounces each) diced tomatoes**

⅓   **cup chopped parsley**

8   **cups water, or 6 cups water and 2 cups white wine**

Ingredients continue on next page

1. In a very large pot, such as a stockpot, heat the oil. Add the leeks, garlic, bell pepper, and celery. Cook over medium heat until the vegetables are softened, about 10 minutes. Add the fennel seed, red pepper flakes, turmeric, and thyme and cook, stirring, for 1 minute. Add the tomatoes, parsley, and water or water and wine. Bring to a boil, reduce the heat, and simmer for about 15 minutes to blend flavors. (The base can be made up to a day ahead and refrigerated. Reheat gently before proceeding.)

Continued on next page

24 clams, scrubbed	**2.** Add the clams and mussels and cook over medium heat, covered, until the shells begin to open, about 5 minutes. Add the fish and simmer until it is cooked through and all the clam and mussel shells are completely open, about 5 more minutes. Season with salt and pepper to taste before serving.
24 mussels, scrubbed	
2½ pounds lean white-fish, cut in chunks (haddock, cod, pollock, or a combination of fish)	
Salt and freshly ground black pepper	8 main-course servings

PILOT CRACKER SURVIVAL

A direct descendant of ship's biscuit, or hardtack, Crown Pilots are large, rectangular, unsalted crackers with some heft and weight and a creamy, neutral flavor. While some Yankees are fond of the small oyster crackers in their chowder, most northern New Englanders define Crown Pilots as a necessary accompaniment to (and sometimes thickener for) chowder.

A few years ago, when Nabisco threatened to discontinue Crown Pilots, the possibility made headline news in the region. "Nabisco May Crack Down on Crown Pilots." "Losing the Pilot." "Crown Pilotless?" Yankees were inspired to rise up en masse, and in a grassroots movement that became known as the "cracker crusade," they petitioned the company to reconsider the decision. And they did.

Lenny & Joe's Fish Tale

Westbrook, Connecticut

From Lenny & Joe's
FRESH FRENCH-FRIED ZUCCHINI
(PAGE 37)
SEMI-CLEAR CLAM CHOWDER
(PAGE 56)
CLASSIC HOT BUTTERED LOBSTER
ROLL (PAGE 104)

Step through the doors of Lenny & Joe's Fish Tale on Route 1 in Westbrook in eastern Connecticut and you feel that unmistakable energy and positive vibe — not to mention smell the mouth-watering aromas — identifying it as one of those truly successful establishments. Everything works here, thanks to owners Lenny and Joe Goldberg and their attention to detail. Slide into a booth, put yourself in the hands of your experienced, friendly waitress, and settle in to peruse the extensive menu.

With the exception of some salads and a couple of steak and chicken dishes, this place is all seafood all the time. Start with a cup of their classic and uniquely full-of-flavor clam chowder or a plate of clams or oysters on the half shell, or steamers with butter and broth, or jumbo shrimp cocktail, or fried calamari, or crab cakes. You can't improve on a lunch of one of Lenny and Joe's seafood rolls.

Shuckin' Oysters

Lenny & Joe's Fish Tale

I love their unpretentious yet absolutely outstanding Hot Buttered Lobster Roll, and all the fried seafood rolls and platters (strip or belly clams, scallops, shrimp, or oysters) are wonderful options. Lenny and Joe also offer a full panoply of broiled seafood — scrod, sole, catfish, scallops, salmon — and on one recent spring day, the daily special was that increasingly rare treat, filleted Connecticut River shad, broiled simply to bring out its sweet, wild flavor. Portions are huge, so plan to share.

Happily, the Fish Tale is open year-round, so if you're craving a hit of summer in the off-season, this is the place.

J's Seafood Bouillabaisse on Pasta

All heads swivel to follow the waitress when she bears bowls of this magnificent bouillabaisse from the kitchen at J's Oyster Bar in Portland, Maine. The seafood stew is simply gorgeous — and tastes simply fabulous — and it makes an impressive main course for entertaining. The servings are huge at J's, so I've scaled this back just a bit for the home cook.

6	tablespoons butter
4	garlic cloves, finely chopped
1	red bell pepper, chopped
1	green bell pepper, chopped
⅓	cup slivered fresh basil
1	teaspoon dried oregano
2	cups dry white wine
12	soft-shell clams, scrubbed
12	mussels, scrubbed
6	sea scallops
6	large shrimp
1½	cups cooked lobster meat, cut in large chunks
½	cup crabmeat
½	pound haddock fillet, cut in 4 pieces

Ingredients continue on next page

1. In a very large, deep skillet with a lid, heat the butter. Add the garlic and bell peppers and cook over medium heat until the peppers begin to soften, about 5 minutes. Add the basil, oregano, and wine and bring to a boil. Cook, uncovered, until the liquid is reduced by about one-third, about 3 minutes. (This base can be made up to 1 day ahead and refrigerated. Reheat before proceeding.)

2. Add the clams and mussels; bring to a boil. Cook, covered, over medium-high heat until the shells begin to open, about 5 minutes. Add the scallops, shrimp, lobster, crabmeat, and haddock. Bring the liquid

Continued on next page

1½ cups good-quality bottled marinara sauce

Salt and freshly ground black pepper

1 pound seashell-shaped pasta

½ cup chopped parsley

Parmesan cheese, optional

to a boil again, reduce the heat, and cook, covered, until the shrimp is pink and the scallops and haddock are opaque, about 3 minutes. Add the marinara sauce to the pot, shake the pan gently to incorporate, and simmer for about 5 minutes to blend flavors. Season with salt and pepper to taste.

3. Meanwhile, bring a large pot of salted water to the boil. Cook the pasta al dente, 8 to 10 minutes. Drain into a colander.

4. Pour the pasta onto a large, deep serving platter and spoon the seafood and sauce over the top. Sprinkle with parsley and pass the Parmesan cheese at the table if desired.

6 to 8 main-course servings

LINGUIÇA AND CHOURICO

Linguiça (pronounced "ling-gweese-ah") and chourico (pronounced "shore-eese") are cured Portuguese pork sausages redolent of garlic and paprika. Hot and spicy, chourico is usually about 1½ to 2 inches in diameter. Linguiça is milder and thinner. These two glorious sausages are a cornerstone of many of the wonderful dishes contributed by the Portuguese, who have been in New England since the 1800s. In Rhode Island and South Coast Massachusetts, the sausages rival hot dogs and hamburgers in popularity. They are eaten with eggs at breakfast; they're served broiled or fried with fried potatoes at diners for lunch; they are the essential ingredient in *caldo verde*, the Portuguese kale soup (see page 77); they enliven and enrich the filling of some of the best baked stuffed clams; and they are added to cheesecloth bags of corn and potatoes at local clambakes. Street fairs and festivals feature huge rafts of linguiça and chourico cooking on open-air grills, sending their garlicky fragrance out to entice all potential attendees. (See Mail-Order Sources, page 240.)

Corn Chowder

When Lee White, a restaurant critic for a northeastern Connecticut newspaper, raved on to me about the Sea Swirl, a clam shack in Mystic, Connecticut, she said, "Their fried food is fabulous, but what I love to eat here more than anything else is their corn chowder." When you read the recipe, you'll see why. This is not your run-of-the-mill, thrown-together corn chowder, but one made with extreme care and top-quality ingredients, including fresh corn, slab bacon, and lobster stock. No wonder Lee loves it so!

6	ears fresh sweet corn
2	live 1-pound lobsters
1	tablespoon salt
¼	pound country slab bacon
4	sprigs fresh thyme plus 2 tablespoons chopped fresh thyme
1	teaspoon whole black peppercorns
2	bay leaves
	Coarse salt
2	tablespoons unsalted butter
2	medium onions, diced
1	teaspoon Hungarian paprika
1	pound all-purpose potatoes, peeled and cut into ½- to ¾-inch dice
1	cup heavy cream
	Freshly ground black pepper

1. Bring a large pot of water to a boil. Husk the corn, remove the silk, and boil until just tender, less than 5 minutes. Drain. When cool, stand the corn vertically on its end on a cutting board and cut off the kernels. Reserve. (Or use 3 cups frozen corn kernels.)

2. Bring about 2 inches of water to a boil in a large pot. Add the lobsters and the 1 tablespoon of salt, cover the pot, and steam until the lobsters turn bright red and the tail meat is no longer translucent, 10 to 15 minutes. Drain. When cool enough to handle, remove the meat and set it aside for another lobster dish (such as the Harraseeket Classic Lobster Rolls, see page 96). Split the carcasses in half and pull out and discard the sandy sacs in the head. Leave about half of the green tomalley in the bodies to flavor the stock.

3. Remove the rind from the bacon and reserve the rind and the bacon separately. Place the lobster shells and carcasses in a large stockpot and cover with 2 quarts of water. Bring to a boil. Add the thyme sprigs, peppercorns, bay leaves, and the piece of bacon rind to the stock. Reduce the heat and simmer, partially covered, for 1 hour. Add the coarse salt to taste and simmer for up to 30 minutes longer to concentrate flavor. Strain the stock, discarding the solids. You should have 4 cups; if not, add water to make up the difference. (See Note.)

Continued on next page

Chowder Anytime

"FISHIEST OF ALL FISHY PLACES

[on Nantucket] was the try pots, which well deserves its name; for the pots there were always boiling chowders. Chowder for breakfast, and chowder for dinner and chowder for supper, till you begin to look for fish bones coming through your clothes."

— **Herman Melville**
on Nantucket chowder, *Moby-Dick*, 1851

4. Cut the reserved bacon into ½-inch dice. In a large soup pot, cook the bacon over medium-low heat until crisp and browned, about 15 minutes. Spoon off all but about 1 tablespoon of fat, leaving the bacon pieces in the pot. Add the butter, onions, and chopped thyme and cook for about 8 minutes, until the onions are tender but not browned. Stir in the paprika. Add the potatoes, corn, and lobster stock. Bring to a boil, reduce the heat to medium, and cook, covered, until the potatoes are tender, 15 to 20 minutes. The potatoes should break up and release some of their starch, lightly thickening the chowder. Remove the pot from the heat.

5. Add the cream. Season with pepper to taste. Let stand off the heat for 30 minutes to 1 hour. (The chowder can be made ahead and refrigerated for 1 day.) Reheat gently and serve.

NOTE: You can substitute 2 cups clam juice and 2 cups water for the lobster stock.

6 first-course servings

Shaw's Fish and Lobster Wharf

New Harbor, Maine

From Shaw's
MILKY MAINE STEAMER CHOWDER (PAGE 61)
LOBSTER STEW (PAGE 75)
LAZY MAN'S LOBSTER (PAGE 123)
LOBSTER POT PIE (PAGE 179)

Shaw's is the kind of large, well-established place whose reputation precedes it. Located on the Pemaquid peninsula in New Harbor, a classic Maine fishing village, Shaw's setting just might be one of the most fascinating on the coast, for the restaurant abuts the working lobster wharf where much of the day's catch is unloaded. As you sit sipping your wine, you can watch the boats tie up and listen to the fishermen banter back and forth as they

off-load your soon-to-be dinner. The protocol at Shaw's is in-the-rough style, meaning you line up to place your order at a counter and then take a seat at one of the picnic tables on the big screened-in deck. The extensive menu offers something for everyone and includes steamers with drawn butter, chowders, a pristine, buttery lobster stew, all manner of seafood rolls, complete shore dinners, a rich and creamy Crumb-Topped Lobster Pie, and their perennially popular Lazy Man's Lobster (fresh-picked meat drizzled with melted butter). All seafood except scallops, which come from New Bedford, is purchased from local fishermen, many of whom work exclusively for Shaw's. For non–fish fanciers and kids, hot dogs, hamburgers, chicken, and steak are on the menu.

SEAFOOD FESTIVALS

If you were so inclined, you could spend all of a summer and most of the fall wandering coastal New England from one seafood festival to the next.

You could begin in early June at the Portsmouth, New Hampshire, Chowder Festival, where they dish out 500 gallons of chowders of all varieties. Then in the first week of July, there's the Chowderfest portion of Boston's Harborfest, where major restaurants from the greater Boston area compete for the distinction of receiving the award for best chowder in New England. Traveling west in the Bay State will bring you in early July to the Great New Bedford Summerfest, where more than 5,000 pounds of seafood are served up in the form of clam cakes, fried fish, and scallops, and some wonderful Portuguese dishes. Moving over to Rhode Island, the town of Warren holds an annual Quahog Festival in mid-July, where the bivalve is featured in countless variations of chowders, fritters, and stuffies. In August, if you move up the coast to Yarmouth, Maine, you'll encounter the yearly Clam Festival, and then it would be on to Rockland for the Lobster Festival, which features the crustaceans boiled and stuffed, and in lobster salad, rolls, and stews. In September, the festivities continue with an Oyster Festival in Norwalk, Connecticut, and then it's back up the coast to Massachusetts to the Scallop Festival in Bourne, the Seafood Festival in Gloucester, and the Clam Fest in Essex. Finally, before the last leaves fall from the trees, check out the Waterfront Seafood Festival in Newport, Rhode Island, in October.

Lobster Stew

Lobster stew is the essence of honest, plain-spoken Yankee cooking — no gimmicks, no tricks, it just is what it is, and that is chunks of lobster meat swimming in buttery milk, seasoned with nothing more than paprika, salt, and pepper. There are two secrets to making a good lobster stew. One is to use the freshest, most recently caught lobsters you can find — and at Shaw's Fish and Lobster Wharf in New Harbor, Maine, that's certainly not a problem, because the seafood is brought in fresh to their own dock every day. The other secret is to make sure that the stew steeps overnight, so that the lobster flavor infuses it fully.

4	live 1½-pound lobsters
½	cup (1 stick) butter
½	teaspoon paprika
½	teaspoon dry mustard
5	cups half-and-half
Salt and freshly ground black pepper	

1. Boil or steam the lobsters in or over boiling salted water until the tail meat is no longer translucent, about 15 minutes. Drain. When cool enough to handle, crack the claws and tail, extract the meat, and cut it into chunks no smaller than ¼ inch. Try to catch and save the lobster juices.

2. In a large saucepan, melt the butter with the paprika and mustard over medium heat, stirring to dissolve the seasonings. Add the lobster meat and any saved juices and cook, stirring, for about 3 minutes. Add the half-and-half and bring just to the simmer. Do not boil. Season with salt and pepper to taste. Refrigerate for at least 24 hours or for up to 2 days.

3. When ready to serve, warm the stew over low heat, stirring frequently, just until it is heated through. Taste and correct the seasonings if necessary, and serve.

8 first-course servings;
4 main-course servings

Maine She-Crab Soup

A few years ago, Myles Henry thought she-crab soup would be an excellent addition to the Maine Diner menu. (The "she" referring to the fact that in the South, where it was invented, crab roe is added to the soup.) "Why not use our great Maine crabmeat in a soup?" reasoned Myles. Local patrons were slightly wary at first, but Myles won them over by handing out free samples — "it was just a matter of getting them hooked" — and now he wouldn't dare take it off the menu.

1	cup bottled clam juice
4	cups whole milk
2	cups half-and-half
3 to 4	tablespoons cornstarch
½	pound fresh lump crabmeat
½	cup dry sherry
1	tablespoon Old Bay seasoning

1. In a small saucepan, bring the clam juice to a boil over high heat. Reduce the heat to medium and cook until the liquid is reduced by about half, 3 to 4 minutes. Reserve.

2. In a large saucepan, combine the milk and half-and-half. Place over medium heat and heat to 185°F, or just until small bubbles form a skin on the surface. Do not boil. In a small bowl, dissolve 3 tablespoons cornstarch with about 3 tablespoons water. Whisk into the hot milk, return to medium heat, and cook until the milk is lightly thickened and creamy. Whisk in the reduced clam juice. If you want it thicker, dissolve the remaining tablespoon cornstarch with a little liquid and stir into the soup.

3. Add the crabmeat, sherry, and Old Bay and cook over gentle heat for 5 minutes.

Makes 4 to 6 first-course servings

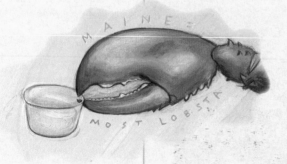

Kale Soup

Kale soup has become such a menu staple in Cape Cod environs that you'd think it had come over on the Mayflower instead of with Portuguese settlers in the nineteenth century. There are as many versions as there are cooks to insist that theirs is the only way it should ever be made, although all would agree that the spicy linguiça sausage is essential. This is the rendition of kale soup that the chef brews up at Land Ho! in Orleans. They age it for two days, but they tell me that some customers will eat the soup only when it's been "cured" even longer!

½   **pound dried red kidney beans (see Note)**

¼   **cup olive oil**

1   **large onion, chopped**

2   **garlic cloves, minced**

2   **cups beef of chicken broth**

1   **can (14 ounces) diced stewed tomatoes**

3   **cups water**

3   **cups diced boiling potatoes, such as red-skinned (about 1 pound)**

½   **pound kale, thinly sliced crosswise**

½   **pound linguiça sausage, thinly sliced**

½   **teaspoon celery salt**

¼   **teaspoon each freshly ground black pepper and white pepper**

¾   **cup finely diced green bell pepper**

Salt

1. If you have time, soak the beans in water to cover for 4 hours or overnight. (See Note.) Drain into a colander. Bring a large pot of water to boil, add 1 teaspoon salt and the soaked or unsoaked beans. Return to a boil, cover, reduce the heat to low, and simmer until the beans are tender, 1 to 2 hours. Drain.

2. In a large soup pot, heat the oil. Add the onion and cook over medium heat until the onion begins to soften, about 5 minutes. Add the garlic and cook for 1 minute. Add the broth, tomatoes, water, and potatoes, bring to a boil, reduce heat to low, and cook covered for 10 minutes. Add the kale, linguiça, celery salt, and both peppers and cook until the potatoes and kale are tender, about 10 minutes longer. Stir in the bell pepper and season with salt to taste. (Salt may not be necessary because the sausage and broth can be salty.) Cool the soup and refrigerate for at least 4 hours or up to 2 days.

3. Reheat gently, adding more liquid and adjusting the seasonings if necessary, and serve.

NOTE: You may substitute 4 cups drained canned kidney beans for the dried beans. It is not necessary to presoak dried beans, although they cook a bit more evenly if you do.

8 to 10 first-course servings; 4 main-course servings.

CHAPTER 4

Top-Loaded Seafood Rolls and Other Sandwiches

When Spenser, private-eye hero of Robert B. Parker's Boston-based detective novels, invites a California girl to lunch at a Boston eatery, she sees "lobster roll" on the menu and asks him what it is. "Is it a kind of sushi or what?" Spenser answers that it's lobster salad on a hot dog roll. When the food arrives, the Californian says, "The lobster's in a damn hot dog roll." "I told you." "Yeah, but I didn't think you meant an actual hot dog roll." It does appear surprising and peculiar to non–New Englanders, this practice of stuffing butter-grilled top-split (sometimes called *top-loaded*) frankfurter rolls or hamburger buns with seafood salad — or more eccentric yet, filling the rolls to overflowing with deep-fried clams, shrimp, oysters, or scallops. I've never actually witnessed a person pick up a deep-fried seafood roll and eat the whole thing. It's just not physically possible. More commonly, the top two-thirds of the fried fish are eaten with the fingers after first being daintily dunked in tartar sauce. The final step is to squeeze any remaining tartar sauce over the last of the seafood, whereupon the sandwich is hoisted up and polished off. A most delicious invention, whatever they're stuffed with.

Grilled Salmon Sandwich

Although the menu at Cape Cod's Captain Frosty's changes very little from year to year (which is a major part of its charm), every now and then owner Pat Henderson adds a new item. This lovely grilled salmon sandwich on sourdough bread was introduced fairly recently, and it's been terrifically successful.

½ cup bottled citrus vinaigrette, or oil and vinegar dressing

1 teaspoon soy sauce

¼ cup prepared mayonnaise

1 heaping tablespoon whole-grain Dijon mustard

2 salmon fillets, about 6 ounces each

4 large slices sourdough bread

Softened butter

Green leaf lettuce

Tomato slices

1. In a small dish, combine the citrus vinaigrette and soy sauce. In another small dish, stir together the mayonnaise and mustard. Set aside.

2. Oil the grill of a charcoal or gas grill. Build a moderately hot charcoal fire or preheat the gas grill. Place the salmon on the grill and cook for 2 to 3 minutes, until browned on one side. Turn and brush generously with the citrus-soy mixture. Cook for 2 to 3 minutes until browned. Turn, brush once more, and continue to cook for a few minutes longer or until the fish is no longer translucent in its thickest part.

3. Place the bread around the cooler edges of the grill and toast lightly. Spread the toast with butter and then with the mustard mayonnaise.

4. Place the salmon on the toast, add lettuce and tomato, cut in half, and serve.

2 servings

Scallop Roll

After a few lean years when scallops began to get scarce, the scallops are back, the scallops are back! At Captain Frosty's on Cape Cod, Pat Henderson pays a premium for local Cape day-boat, dry-packed scallops — which means they haven't been soaked or processed with preservative. She insists on small, uniformly sized "seas," so they cook evenly in the fryer, and she then heaps the sweet, golden-crusted beauties into butter-grilled rolls.

Canola or other vegetable oil for frying

1 cup breading mix (see Notes)

⅓ cup evaporated milk

⅔ cup water

10 ounces small sea scallops

2 New England–style top-split hot dog rolls

Softened butter

Lemon wedges

Tartar sauce

1. Heat the oil over medium heat in a deep fryer or deep pot until it reaches 365°F (see Notes).

2. Place the breading mix in a medium bowl. In another medium bowl, whisk together the evaporated milk and water. Roll the scallops in the breading and toss well to coat. Transfer to the milk mixture and toss to coat. Return the scallops to the breading mix and, using your hands, make sure each scallop is evenly coated. Transfer to a colander or large strainer and shake gently to remove excess breading.

3. Slide the scallops into the hot oil and fry until golden brown, 2 to 3 minutes. Drain on paper towels.

4. Meanwhile, heat a griddle or cast iron skillet over medium-high heat. Spread the cut outsides of the rolls with butter and grill, buttered-sides down, until golden, 2 to 3 minutes.

5. Stuff the scallops into the grilled rolls and serve with lemon wedges and tartar sauce.

NOTES: At Captain Frosty's, they use a commercial breading mix that contains corn flour, white flour, salt, leavening, nonfat milk, and powdered eggs.

You could also shallow-fry the scallops in ½ to ¾ inch of oil. (See Frying Basics, page 146.)

2 servings

Grilled Cheese Sandwiches with Tomato

When I asked my friend Elinor Klivans if she'd divulge the name of her favorite clam shack/lobster pound in her part of Maine, her unreserved recommendation was Cod End in Tenants Harbor. She said, "We go so often that sometimes we end up just getting the grilled cheese on anadama bread with tomatoes. It's outstanding, and the perfect lunch when you're not in the mood for seafood." The secret, of course, is to start with good bread — Cod End gets their oatmeal and molasses anadama from the Schoolhouse Bakery in town — and to use a nice, sharp (preferably Vermont) Cheddar cheese.

4 thick slices Cape Ann Anadama Bread (see page 84) or other bread of choice, such as any whole-grain bread

2 to 3 tablespoons softened butter, plus additional if necessary

4 ounces sharp white Cheddar, thinly sliced

1 tomato, thinly sliced

1. Heat a griddle or cast-iron frying pan over medium heat. Spread the bread with the butter. Place two slices of the bread buttered-side down in the pan. (If the pan is not well seasoned, you may need to grease it with some butter.)

2. Layer the cheese over the bread, then layer with the tomato slices and top with the remaining two pieces of bread, buttered-sides up. Cook, pressing with a large spatula to flatten slightly, until browned on the bottom and the cheese begins to melt, about 2 minutes. Turn and cook another 2 to 3 minutes or until the second side is browned and the cheese is melted and hot.

3. Cut the sandwiches in half on the diagonal; serve.

2 servings

Cape Ann Anadama Bread

The legend (probably apocryphal, but a good story) is that a woman named Anna, who lived on Cape Ann, Massachusetts, was such a poor cook that all she could seem to produce was a paltry paste of cornmeal and molasses. One day, her long-suffering and very hungry fisherman husband began throwing yeast and flour into her bowl of gruel, all the while muttering under his breath, "Anna, damn her!" Thus was born the classic cornmeal and molasses anadama loaf — moist, dark, full of flavor — and the bread of choice for a Cod End grilled cheese sandwich.

½   **cup yellow cornmeal, plus 2 teaspoons**

2   **teaspoons salt**

4   **tablespoons butter, cut in pieces**

1   **cup boiling water**

¼   **cup molasses**

1   **package regular yeast (see Note)**

¼   **cup hot tap water (105 to 115°F)**

2½ to 3 cups **all-purpose flour, preferably unbleached**

1. In a large mixing bowl or in the bowl of a standing electric mixer, combine ½ cup of the cornmeal and the salt and butter. Add the boiling water and the molasses, and stir until the butter melts. Set aside for 15 minutes to let the cornmeal soften.

2. In a small bowl, dissolve the yeast in the hot tap water and let stand for about 10 minutes.

3. Stir the yeast mixture into the cornmeal mixture. Add 2 cups of the flour and stir with a wooden spoon to mix well. Add ½ cup additional flour and knead by hand on a well-floured board or with the dough hook attachment of a mixer until the dough is smooth and elastic, about 10 minutes by hand or about 5 minutes by machine. Continue to add flour as necessary to achieve a fairly firm but workable dough. Leave in the mixer bowl or transfer the dough to a greased bowl, cover, and let rise until doubled in bulk, about 1½ hours.

Continued on next page

WHY HE DOES IT

Steve Kingston, owner of The Clam Shack in Kennebunkport, Maine, discusses his reasons for loving the clam shack business. "First and foremost, I have always just plain loved fried clams. I still do. And I get totally energized on a busy Saturday when it's super busy and everything's humming and we're all working as a team. And our kitchen is close to the take-out window, so we can hear customers' comments and compliments, we can thank them, tease them . . . there's nothing like that close contact."

4. Butter a 9- by 5-inch loaf pan and sprinkle the bottom and sides with 1 teaspoon of the remaining cornmeal. Punch the dough down, shape into a loaf, and place in the prepared pan. Cover lightly and set aside until almost doubled in bulk, 45 minutes to 1 hour.

5. Preheat the oven to 400°F. Sprinkle the top of the loaf with the remaining teaspoon of cornmeal. Bake in the center of the preheated oven for 10 minutes. Reduce the oven temperature to 350°F and continue to bake for 35 to 40 minutes, or until the top is rich golden brown and the loaf sounds hollow when tapped on the bottom.

6. Remove from the pan and cool completely on a wire rack before slicing. (The bread can be sealed in a plastic bag and frozen. Thaw in the wrapping before using.)

NOTE: Quick-rise yeast can be substituted. Rising times will be about half as long.

Makes 1 large loaf

Captain Frosty's

Dennis, Massachusetts

From Captain Frosty's

GRILLED SALMON SANDWICH (P...
SCALLOP ROLL (PAGE 81)
ORANGE FREEZE (PAGE 210)

It looks like the quintessential spiffy '50s-style dairy bar — and it is. But Captain Frosty's is also one of Cape Cod's very best clam shacks, with a complete menu of all the expected fried seafood rolls and plates, as well as a few "modern" additions, such as a truly delicious grilled salmon sandwich and a juicy Black Angus hand-ground beef burger that a much-traveled hamburger aficionado pronounces "the best on

the Cape." Captain Frosty's has been owned and run by Pat and Mike Henderson since 1976, and they are in almost constant attendance, personally overseeing this busy, friendly, and efficient operation. After placing your order at the inside counter, take a seat at one of the tables indoors or head back to a leaf-shaded outdoor patio or to one of the picnic tables on the side. A smiling waitress brings your tray, heaped with some of the finest food you'll find anywhere. All the fish is from Chatham and is hooked rather than gill-netted, which means it is fresher and tastier. Their scallops are day-boat caught and never processed with preservatives, and their sweet whole-belly clams are local.

Onion rings are hand-cut, and all frying is done in super-clean canola oil. The Hendersons, who are originally from Rhode Island, introduced clam cakes (fritters) to Cape Cod, and theirs are light and chock-full of clams. After your meal, head around front to the separate ice cream window and order a little something sweet for dessert — perhaps a refreshing Orange Freeze or chocolate "frappe" (a New England term for milk shake).

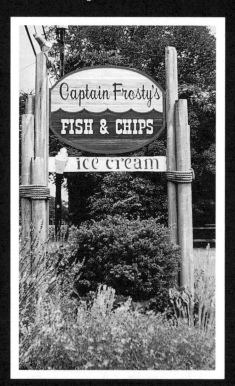

Crabmeat Roll

When I asked Judy Astbury, owner of Bagaduce Lunch in Penobscot, Maine, for her crab roll recipe, she said, "It's so simple, maybe it will be disappointing. I don't put much in it because what I like to taste is the pure, sweet crabmeat." That, in a nutshell, just about sums up the philosophy of all successful clam shack cooks.

¾ **pound fresh lump-style crabmeat, picked over**

About ½ cup mayonnaise (see Note)

Salt and freshly ground black pepper

4 **soft hamburger buns, split**

2 **tablespoons butter, softened**

Boston or butter lettuce leaves, optional

Tomato slices, optional

1. In a bowl, combine the crabmeat with enough mayonnaise to bind the salad, stirring gently but thoroughly to blend. Season with salt and pepper to taste. Refrigerate the salad if not using immediately.

2. Spread the insides of the rolls with butter and grill, cut-side down, on a cast-iron griddle or frying pan until lightly toasted.

3. Heap the crab salad on the buns, top with a lettuce leaf and tomato slices, if desired, and serve.

NOTE: At Bagaduce, they use Kraft mayonnaise.

4 servings

Clam Shack Advice

"NO DIETERS ALLOWED! If you don't like fried food, this is probably not the place for you."

— **Judy Astbury**
Bagaduce Lunch

GONE CLAMMIN'

Clams are getting somewhat scarce along the New England coast, but there are still plenty of local flats where you can dig yourself a bucketful. Here are some essentials.

- Ask around locally and find out which flats are open, and inquire about the rules and regulations governing clamming in that area.

- Get yourself a permit, if required.

- Acquire the proper tools. For soft-shell clams, use a short-handled rake. For hard-shells, you'll need a long-handled rake. Some diggers prefer a shovel.

- Take along a bucket or basket or two.

- To find clams, look on clam flats at low tide for small, uniform holes on the surface of the sand or mud. Clams make these holes when they expel water. Sometimes they squirt water right out of the sand. Tiny holes indicate quahogs, which live less than 6 inches under the surface. Larger holes are a sure sign of steamers, which live a foot or more under the surface.

- Try to walk softly on the flats, and when you dig, dig fast. A clam alerted to imminent danger is capable of a rapid descent down or sideways to avoid being captured.

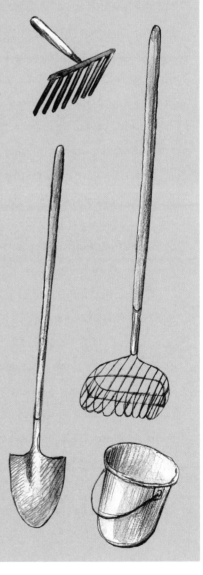

FRYING LAWS, ACCORDING TO SKIP ATWOOD

Skip Atwood is a fried-food fanatic and guru to an entire generation of clam shack cooks. Skip was the owner/manager of the Clam Box in Ipswich, Massachusetts, for 10 years, where he learned good frying technique from the original owner, and then went further by establishing the highest possible standards for fried-food excellence. Some of Skip's frying laws are as follows:

"The quality of the clams is first and foremost. Hot-dipping (which makes clams easier to shuck) makes clams tough, and they lose some of their flavor.

"I prefer breading to battering. Battering adds too much starch to the seafood taste, although I have had some very good battered clams.

"I like to roll my clams in evaporated milk and then in a three-to-one mixture of corn flour and pastry flour. The pastry flour is sticky, allowing the corn flour to adhere better. I toss my clams and fish back and forth like a hot potato to shake off any excess breading. The breading must be sifted after a few batches because it develops clumps from the milk that the clams are dipped in.

"Good deep fryers are key. They must be well maintained and checked regularly to make sure there are no cold spots. They must be big enough to maintain a temperature of 365°F when large quantities of food are dropped in. I always have one or two back-up fryers in case of a problem.

"Everyone has a favorite frying medium. I think it matters more that the oil be clean than what it is. Some use canola oil, some use a meat/vegetable [oil] blend, some use lard. It should be something with a higher smoking point, so the food cooks quickly on the outside, leaving the inside juicy.

"A lot of cars in a parking lot is a sure sign that a restaurant is moving a lot of product, so the seafood should be good and fresh."

Fried Cod Sandwich

Sea Swirl owner Dave Blaney goes down to the docks in Stonington, Connecticut, every single day in the summer to get his fish, including the freshest possible cod for his spectacular fish sandwich.

Soybean oil for frying

½   **cup dry batter mix (see Note)**

½   **cup lukewarm water, plus additional table-spoons if necessary**

2   **pieces fresh cod, approximately 3½ inches square and ½-inch thick, 6 to 8 ounces each**

2   **hamburger buns, lightly toasted**

Lettuce leaves and sliced tomatoes, optional

1. Pour the oil into a deep fryer, filling no more than about half full, or into a large skillet to a depth of ½ inch. Heat over medium heat to 375°F. (See Note.)

2. In a mixing bowl, whisk together the batter mix and the water until smooth, adding a bit more water if necessary to make a batter about the consistency of thick buttermilk. Dry the fish well on paper towels. Dip the fish into the batter, then let excess batter drip off. Slide into the hot fat and cook, turning once, until the batter is golden brown and the fish is opaque, about 5 minutes.

3. Place the fish on the buns, add the lettuce and tomatoes, if desired, and serve.

NOTE: Sea Swirl uses Fis-Chic, a premium breading mix made in Warwick, Rhode Island, by Drum Rock Specialty Co., Inc., which also makes a Fritter and Clam Cake Mix. (See Mail-Order Sources, page 240.) Fis-Chic contains flour, corn flour, whey, baking powder, and salt. Many brands of dry batter mix are available in the supermarket; look for one with similar ingredients.

You could shallow-fry the fish in ½ to ¾ inch of oil. (See Frying Basics, page 146.)

2 servings

Fried Clam Roll

The fried clams at The Clam Shack in Kennebunkport, Maine, are among the best I've ever eaten, and after talking with owner Steve Kingston and listening to his passionate dissertation on achieving fried clam perfection, I'm not surprised that the result is so extraordinary. It goes without saying that he starts with the very best clams (and his purveyors know that he'll return them if they're not up to his standards), makes his own breading mix from scratch, uses a high-quality frying oil that gets changed twice a day in season, and, for the toasted clam roll, insists on a smear of real butter instead of margarine. This close approximation adapted for the home cook makes four full-to-overflowing clam rolls.

Solid white shortening for frying, such as Crisco

2 pints shucked medium-sized soft-shell clams

½ cup whole milk

½ cup cold water

2 teaspoons clam liquor or bottled clam juice

1 cup yellow corn flour (see Note)

1 cup bleached all-purpose flour

2 teaspoons salt

½ teaspoon freshly ground black pepper

4 top-split hot dog buns

2 tablespoons melted butter

Tartar sauce

Lemon wedges

1. Heat the shortening over medium heat in a deep fryer or deep pot until the shortening is melted and reaches 375°F.

2. Cut the necks (siphons) off the clams and rinse them gently if they are muddy.

3. In a medium bowl, combine the milk, water, and clam liquor. In a large bowl, stir or whisk together the corn flour, all-purpose flour, salt, and pepper.

4. Using your hands, dip about one-third of the clams into the milk wash. Let the excess liquid drain off. Dredge the clams in the breading mix, using your hands to make sure each clam is evenly coated. Transfer to a colander or large strainer and shake gently to remove excess breading.

5. Slide the clams into the hot fat and deep-fry until they are golden brown, 1 to 2 minutes. Drain on paper towels. Repeat with the remaining clams. (The cooked clams can be kept warm in a slow oven for 10 to 15 minutes.)

6. Meanwhile, heat a griddle or cast-iron frying pan over medium-high heat. Brush the crustless sides of

Continued on next page

THE BIRTH OF THE FRIED CLAM AT WOODMAN'S

Here's how the story goes. Lawrence "Chubby" Woodman and his wife, Bessie, had a small concession stand in Essex, Massachusetts, where they sold fruit, chewing gum, homemade potato chips — and steamer clams that Chubby dug every morning out of the famous nearby Ipswich clam flats. One slow, hot July day in 1916, a neighbor suggested (perhaps in jest) that Woodman might try frying up some of his clams. So . . . Bessie conceived of dipping the clams in batter first and then submerging them in the kettle of bubbling lard used to fry their potato chips. Eureka! Customers immediately scarfed down that first batch — and the Woodmans were on their way not only to prosperity but to fried clam immortality.

Today, Woodman's of Essex is a sprawling complex of clam shack/raw bar/gift shop/catering hall. It's still in the same location, still run by the Woodman family, and still acknowledged by all in North Shore clamdom to be the great-granddaddy of all fried clam establishments.

the rolls with melted butter and grill, turning once, until golden, 2 to 3 minutes.

7. Stuff the fried clams into the grilled rolls. Serve with tartar sauce and lemon wedges.

NOTE: Corn flour is finely ground cornmeal. Some "breading mix" is simply pure corn flour or corn flour plus salt. Check labels. Pure corn flour is also available at most health food stores or can be mail-ordered (see page 240). Masa harina, available in many supermarkets in the Spanish foods section, may be substituted.

4 generous servings

The Clam Shack

Kennebunkport, Maine

From The Clam Shack

FRIED CLAM ROLL (PAGE 92)

HADDOCK SANDWICH (PAGE 98)

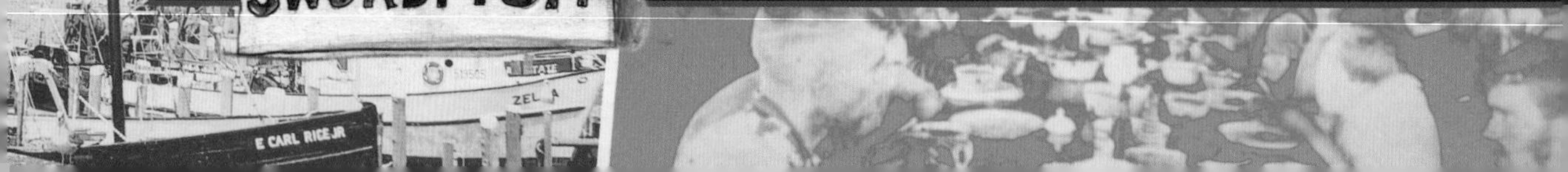

Hanging over the river right at the Kennebunkport bridge, The Clam Shack is about as big as a lobster boat, the parking is challenging, there are no tables at all, but . . . this place does the best fried clams on the entire Maine coast, and, for that reason alone, is more than worth a detour from anywhere. Tourists and locals line up in front all summer long to place their orders for The Clam Shack's lightly breaded, sweet and tender whole-belly fried clams (in rolls or "boxes"), incredibly succulent fried fresh haddock sandwiches, their legendary lobster rolls (mayonnaise or butter option), steamers, sweet onion rings, and about a dozen other menu items. Owner Steve Kingston runs a meticulous operation, demanding nothing but the absolute best-quality ingredients from his purveyors, strict quality control in the cooking of each and every order, and efficiency and friendliness in his employees. This is strictly a walk-away, two-window system, and the staff handles the crowds with speed and grace. When you pick up your tray of goodies, you can perch on or in your car and take in the passing summer parade, meander down to a deck next door, lean over the river to eat, and toss the seagulls a fry or two — or take your order to a nearby beach.

Classic Lobster Roll with Mayo

The lobster rolls at Harraseeket Lunch and Lobster Company in South Freeport, Maine, could well be used as the prototype for all others up and down the Maine coast. There, they make the simplest, chunkiest lobster salad from recently caught and cooked lobsters and pile it into a warm, butter-grilled, top-loaded bun, with the only concession to crunch being the pale green lettuce leaf nestled beneath the salad. That's it — but when the primary ingredients are of the best quality and are handled properly, this sandwich is a bit of nirvana, Maine-style.

4   live 1- to 1¼-pound lobsters

½   cup mayonnaise, plus additional if necessary (see Note)

Salt and freshly ground black pepper

4   New England–style split-top hot dog rolls

4   tablespoons melted butter

4   large leaves green leaf lettuce

1. Bring a large pot of salted water to the boil. Cook the lobsters by boiling or steaming them in or over the water until they turn bright red and the meat is firm and opaque, 10 to 15 minutes. Drain and run under cold water. When the lobsters are cool enough to handle, crack the shells and extract the meat. Cut the meat into chunks no smaller than about ¾ inch. You should have about 5 cups of meat. Refrigerate until cold.

2. In a large bowl, toss the lobster meat with the mayonnaise. Stir gently to combine, adding a bit more mayonnaise if needed to bind the salad. Season with salt and pepper to taste. (The salad can be made up to 6 hours ahead and refrigerated.)

3. Heat a griddle or cast-iron skillet over medium heat. Brush the crustless sides of the rolls with butter, place on the griddle, and toast, turning once, until both sides are golden brown, about 2 minutes per side.

4. Place a lettuce leaf inside each roll, fill with lobster salad, and serve.

NOTE: At Harraseeket, they use Hellmann's mayonnaise (which is Best Foods brand on the West Coast).

4 servings

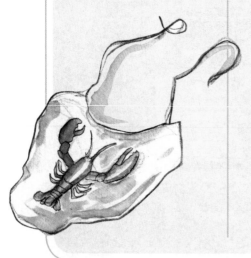

harraseeket
LUNCH
CRABMEAT & LOBSTER ROLLS
Seafood Baskets a Specialty
ICE CREAM • MILK • SODA • COFFEE

NO PICNIC LUNCHES
ALLOWED

TABLES ARE FOR
PATRONS OF

Harraseeket
Lunch & Lobster
ONLY

We

HARRASE

IF YOU A

LOB

STEAMERS.

LOBST

Please

WATE

Haddock Sandwich

Just like everything else at The Clam Shack in Kennebunkport, Maine, the haddock sandwich is without peer, holding up a standard that few other places can match. Owner Steve Kingston buys only the freshest local haddock or day-boat Icelandic fish. And he accepts only fish that weigh more than 1 pound, so he can cull the thick center cut (middle) of the fillet for his sandwiches. (A good many other establishments use the thinner tail portion for their sandwiches.) The breading is his own from-scratch blend, his oil is high quality and fresh, and he serves the crispy, sweet-fleshed fish on a generously sized roll from a local bakery.

Solid vegetable shortening for deep-frying, such as Crisco

½ cup whole milk

½ cup cold water

½ cup corn flour (see Notes)

½ cup bleached all-purpose flour

1 teaspoon salt

¼ teaspoon freshly ground black pepper

2 center-cut haddock fillets, about 4 inches square and ¾-inch thick (6 ounces each)

2 large, good-quality hamburger rolls

1 tablespoon melted butter

6 slices tomato

4 lettuce leaves

1. Heat the shortening over medium heat in a deep fryer or a deep skillet until the fat melts and reaches 375°F. (See Note.)

2. In a shallow dish, combine the milk and water. In another dish, stir or whisk together the corn flour, all-purpose flour, salt, and pepper.

3. Dip the haddock in the milk wash. Let the excess drip off, then dredge in the breading mix, shaking off the excess flour. Repeat by dipping the fish once again into the wash and the breading.

4. Slide the fish into the hot fat and fry until the fish is golden brown on both sides and cooked through, about 3 minutes. Drain on paper towels.

5. Meanwhile, heat a griddle or cast-iron frying pan over medium-high heat. Brush the cut sides of the rolls with melted butter. Grill, buttered-sides down, until golden, 2 to 3 minutes.

Continued on next page

6. Place the fish on the grilled rolls, layer with lettuce and tomato, and serve.

NOTE: Corn flour is finely ground cornmeal. Some "breading mix" is simply pure corn flour or corn flour plus salt. Check labels. Pure corn flour is also available at most health food stores or can be mail-ordered (see page 240). Masa harina, available in many supermarkets in the Spanish foods section, may be substituted.

You could also shallow-fry the fish in ½ to ¾ inch of fat or oil in a heavy skillet. (See Frying Basics, page 146.)

2 servings

A STICKLER FOR THE BEST CLAMS

Steve Kingston, owner of The Clam Shack in Kennebunkport, Maine, explains his clam philosophy: "The whole thing is to start with the best clams — and I mean nothing but the best. We get ours from a supplier we trust, and about half are local Maine clams and the other half come from the Ipswich, Massachusetts, area. Either way, we always get 'native select' grade, which are guaranteed to have a consistent size and taste. We get medium-size clams; too large, and the clams are unpalatable, too small and they get overcooked and dried out too quickly. This is a very labor-intensive grade because first the supplier must cull through for shell size. After he shucks them, he culls through again for belly size, making sure they're uniform. I also insist that the neck always be trimmed off — it's tough and chewy. And I mean it must be well trimmed right down to the edge of the clam — no sloppy cutting for me. I return 'em if so. I know I'm a stickler, but keeping to these high standards is what has made this place so successful all these years — and I take personal pride in carrying on that tradition."

Flo's Clam Shack

Middletown, Rhode Island
Portsmouth, Rhode Island

How did Rhode Island get so lucky that it has *two* Flo's? There's the charming, funky, bi-level warren of dining rooms and decks that is the main restaurant and raw bar in Middletown, *and* a small, weather beaten, truly clam-shacky "annex" in Portsmouth right across from a beach. The original Flo's started in the Portsmouth location in 1936 but then became the target of just about every major hurricane to wallop the New England coast in the twentieth century — starting with Rhode Island's behemoth, the 1938 storm, which completely destroyed their first building. In the 1950s, Flo's was hit by two more giant storms and finally, in 1991, the structure was again washed away by Hurricane Bob. Flo's rebuilt repeatedly at the beach location, and then, in 1992, they also opened the larger place in an only slightly more protected beachy spot in Middletown.

Both are great. The Middletown location has lots of indoor deck seating, where they serve all their great cooked seafood specialties, plus the separate Topside Raw Bar, where you can slurp down a platter of classic typical raw bar favorites — little-necks, oysters, chilled lobster meat, crab claws, peel 'n' eat shrimp — and watch the sun set over Ochre Point. For Flo's famous fried seafood, head downstairs to order the likes of light

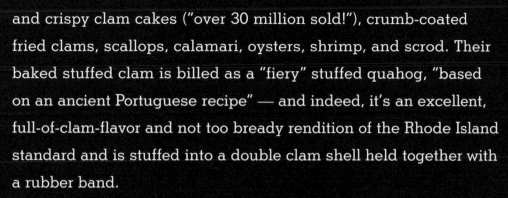

and crispy clam cakes ("over 30 million sold!"), crumb-coated fried clams, scallops, calamari, oysters, shrimp, and scrod. Their baked stuffed clam is billed as a "fiery" stuffed quahog, "based on an ancient Portuguese recipe" — and indeed, it's an excellent, full-of-clam-flavor and not too bready rendition of the Rhode Island standard and is stuffed into a double clam shell held together with a rubber band.

Both Flo's locations have outstanding chowder — clear, creamy, or red — and when you place your order, you're handed a beach rock with your number, which you return when your food is ready. "No rock, no food!" is one of Flo's many instructive (and usually funny) signs.

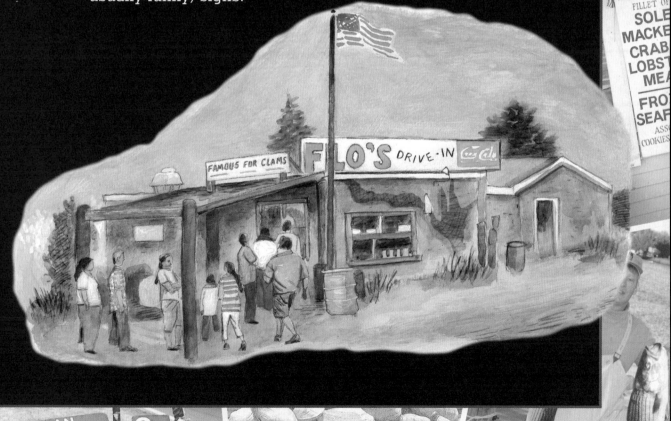

Jenny's Special Sandwich

All the food at Five Islands Lobster Company is great, but their best-selling sandwich by far is the Jenny Special — Jenny being Jenny Butler, who, with husband Chris, runs the place. She came up with the concept for this double-decker affair comprised of sautéed fresh local haddock fillet topped with a Maine crabmeat cake, all layered together with lettuce and tomato in a toasted bun. Yum, Jenny!

½ **pound crabmeat**

Half an egg (see Note)

⅓ **cup mayonnaise**

1½ **teaspoons Dijon mustard**

⅛ **teaspoon cayenne pepper**

Four 4- to 5-ounce haddock fillets

Salt

Freshly ground black pepper

Garlic powder

6 to 9 tablespoons vegetable oil for pan-frying

4 **sesame-seeded hamburger buns, lightly toasted**

4 **leaves green-leaf lettuce**

8 **slices tomato**

4 **wedges fresh lime**

Tartar sauce or other Five Islands–style sauce (see Note with Fresh Salmon Fish and Chips, page 140)

1. In a medium bowl, combine the crabmeat, egg, mayonnaise, mustard, and cayenne. Stir gently but thoroughly to mix.

2. Season the haddock with salt and pepper and sprinkle lightly with garlic powder.

3. You will need two or three frying pans. Pour about 3 tablespoons of oil into each pan and heat over medium-high heat. Using a half-cup measure, scoop out four portions of the crabmeat mixture and spoon into the hot oil. Cook until crusty and brown on both sides, turning carefully, about 6 minutes total. (Due to the lack of starch filler, the cakes will be flatter than the standard crab cake.)

4. Cook the haddock in the oil in other pan(s) until nicely browned on both sides, about 5 minutes.

5. Place haddock on grilled buns and top each with a crab cake. Place lettuce and tomato on the other bun half and serve with lime wedges and tartar sauce or similar sauce on the side.

NOTE: In a small bowl, lightly beat an egg, then scoop out half for the crab cake mixture.

4 servings

ASK - THEN EAT - LOCAL

Find yourself in a town with no books like *The New England Clam Shack Cookbook* to provide insider guidance? You can't necessarily rely on recommendations from your hotel or motel, as they're likely to steer visitors in the direction of the slick, pseudo-fancy spots in town — the kind the Chamber of Commerce might tout. Instead, chat up the locals. Here's your line: "We're looking for a place to go for lunch/supper — nothing fancy or touristy, just good local eating. Got any suggestions?" People love to talk about food. It's the great leveler. Try to get recommendations from a couple of different sources and gather a consensus.

- **If you're staying in a B & B,** ask other guests or your host at breakfast. Or, if you've found a good diner for breakfast, poll customers at the counter or ask the waitresses.

- **If you're lucky enough to have found a farmers' market** in the morning, make inquiries there.

- **If you're in a waterside town,** find the fishing docks or marinas and ask local fishermen where they eat.

- **Carpenters and other working guys** build up powerful appetites. They often know the best — and least expensive — lunch spots in town.

- **Don't be afraid of a little local rowdiness.** Sometimes places that look like divey saloons serve up great "pub grub."

Classic Hot Buttered Lobster Roll

You can find hot buttered lobster rolls in establishments scattered all along the coast, but this pristine, mayonnaise-free variation on the *homarus* sandwich tends to be associated more with southern New England. Westbrook, Connecticut's Lenny & Joe's Fish Tale is an ideal spot to sample this beauty, which is — very simply indeed — lobster claw and tail meat warmed and gilded with clarified butter and then heaped into a grilled top-loaded bun.

10	tablespoons (1 stick plus 2 tablespoons) butter
4	top-split frankfurter rolls
4	cups lobster claw and tail meat cut in approximate 1½-inch chunks

Lemon wedges

1. In a saucepan, melt the butter over low heat. Remove from the heat and let stand for a few minutes, allowing the white milk solids to settle to the bottom. Slowly pour the clear yellow butter fat into another container, leaving the milk solids behind.

2. Heat a griddle or cast-iron frying pan over medium heat. Brush the outsides of the rolls with about 2 tablespoons of the butter and brown on both sides in the preheated pan.

3. In a large skillet over medium to medium-high heat, toss the lobster meat with the remaining butter until just heated through. Heap the buttered lobster into the grilled rolls, garnish with a lemon wedge, and serve.

4 servings

The "Rhode Island Lunch" Sandwich

This is really just a simple (and scrumptious) broiled cheese sandwich sprinkled with some chopped sweet onion and pickle relish. So why does Rhode Island claim it as their own? Well . . . as is the case with most of the Ocean State's idiosyncratic foodways (see Rhode Island's Quirky Cuisine, page 188) — who knows, but why not? I first ate one of these at Flo's in Middletown, but you can find the sandwich at diners and luncheonettes all over the state.

4	hamburger buns
8	slices American cheese
⅓	cup chopped sweet onion, such as Vidalia
⅓	cup sweet pickle relish

1. Preheat the broiler. Open the buns and place two slices of cheese on each bun bottom. Broil both halves of the buns until the cheese melts slightly and the top half of the bun is lightly browned.

2. Sprinkle cheese with onion and relish, close, and serve.

2 to 4 servings

A Perfect Roll

"THE LOBSTER ROLL HAD BEEN PERFECT — plenty of lobster meat, Hellman's mayonnaise, and a little salt and pepper piled on a hot dog roll that had been toasted in butter. No frou-frou ingredients like capers, not even lettuce. It wasn't on . . . any diet but it was sublime."

— Katherine Hall Page
The Body in the Lighthouse

CHAPTER 5

Lobster, Clams, and Other Shellfish

Early New England settlers wrote home with tales of enormous lobsters that could be plucked effortlessly from the beach or sea and of seemingly limitless numbers of bivalves to be gathered from clam, oyster, and scallop beds. The colonists cooked their shellfish simply and straightforwardly, a habit that remains deeply ingrained and is still the routine practice in the region. Hence, the primary mode of cooking lobsters at in-the-rough lobster pounds is to simply boil or steam the crustaceans in or over seawater, though full-service New England shore houses or chowder houses typically include a "lazy man's" lobster to satisfy those customers who aren't interested in taking the "bugs" apart. Likewise, local, freshly dug clams and mussels were (and still often are) simply steamed and served with their steel-gray broth and melted butter — until the commercial deep fryer was perfected in the 1920s, and clam shackers started dipping whole-belly clams (and now calamari and tiny Maine shrimp and just about any other sea-food you can name) in batter and deep-frying them up in kettles of boiling oil.

Fried Clams

Chickie Aggelakis, owner of the Clam Box in Ipswich, has just a couple of basic but unwavering clam rules. She insists that her suppliers provide fresh, whole-belly clams of a uniform, medium size, and the clams must be dry-packed, because too much moisture adversely affects both a fried clam's flavor and its ability to crisp in the fryer. Dale Harrington, who has been with the restaurant for over 30 years, applies a simple breading technique, cooks the clams in high-quality oil (they favor M/V, a commercial meat-vegetable blend), maintaining the proper frying temperature, and changes the oil frequently. The crispy clams, which are a perfect proportion of crust to meat, are heaped onto platters and borne to the window or table.

Vegetable oil or solid white shortening for frying, such as Crisco

2½ pints shucked medium-sized, whole-belly soft-shell clams

1½ cups evaporated milk

1½ cups yellow corn flour (see Note)

¾ cup pastry flour, cake flour, or all-purpose flour

Aggelakis Tartar Sauce (page 185)

Lemon wedges

1. Heat the oil or shortening over medium heat in a deep fryer or heavy, deep pot until it reaches a temperature of 350°F.

2. Rinse the clams gently if they are muddy, and dry on paper towels.

3. Pour the evaporated milk into a large bowl. In another large bowl, stir together the corn flour and pastry flour.

4. Using your hands, dip about one-third of the clams into the milk, letting the excess liquid drain off. Dredge the clams in the flour mixture, using your hands to make sure each clam is evenly coated. Transfer to a colander or large strainer and shake gently to remove the excess flour.

Continued on next page

5. Slide the clams into the hot fat and deep-fry until golden brown, 2 to 4 minutes, depending on the size of the clams. (Cooked clams can be kept warm in a slow oven while you finish the remaining frying.)

6. Serve with tartar sauce and lemon wedges.

NOTE: Corn flour is finely ground cornmeal. Some "breading mix" is simply pure corn flour or corn flour plus salt. Check labels. Pure corn flour is also available at most health food stores or can be mail-ordered (see page 240). Masa harina, available in many supermarkets in the Spanish foods section, may be substituted.

4 servings

HOW TO SHUCK OYSTERS

1. Place the oyster in a folded kitchen towel or oven mitt and hold with the deep, rounded side of the shell down to preserve the juices.

2. To open, use a strong paring knife, a special oyster knife (with pointed blade and protective shield), or the point of a can opener. Insert the point of the knife into the hinge between the shells and pry open. Turn the knife to lift the upper shell. Cut through the hinge muscle.

3. Use the point of the knife to scrape the meat attached to the top shell. Slide the knife blade under the oyster in the bottom shell, trying to preserve as much juice as possible.

4. Place oysters on a bed of cracked or shaved ice if serving on the half shell, or remove from the shell if using for other purposes.

Fried Calamari with Pickled Peppers

Many places in Rhode Island and Massachusetts list calamari on their menus, but I've never had such a good batch as at Champlin's on the Galilee pier in Narragansett, Rhode Island. They buy locally caught and processed whole-body squid (no tentacles — too many customers are squeamish about them), slice them thickly, fry them quickly, and serve up with sliced pickled hot peppers, which are the perfect counterpoint to the rich fried seafood.

Vegetable oil for frying

2 **pounds calamari bodies (see Notes)**

1½ **cups dry breading mix (see Notes)**

½ **cup sliced pickled hot peppers, such as banana peppers or mixed red and green Italian pickled peppers**

1. Heat the oil over medium heat in a deep fryer or large, deep pot to 350°F. (See Note.)

2. Slice the calamari crosswise into rings about ½ inch wide. Dredge the calamari rings in the breading mix, shaking off the excess. Slide about one-quarter of the calamari into the hot oil; cook until golden brown, about 2 minutes. Drain on paper towels, and repeat the process with the remaining squid.

3. Serve accompanied by the pickled peppers.

NOTES: Champlin's uses squid bodies only, but feel free to use the tentacles, too.

For breading mix, Champlin's uses Drum Rock "Fis-Chic," which contains flour, corn flour, whey, baking powder, and salt. (See Mail-Order Sources, page 240.)

If you are making a smaller batch of calamari, you could shallow-fry them in ¾ inch of oil. (See Frying Basics, page 146.)

4 servings

Pan-Grilled Sea Scallops

When Dom Bitto, chef/owner of Evelyn's in Tiverton, Rhode Island, found that one of his seafood suppliers could provide him with large, incredibly fresh, dry-pack scallops, he tried sprinkling them with a little simple seasoning mix and cooking them on his ever-ready grill top — and a new menu item was born. To make these at home, be sure to search out high-grade dry-pack scallops. Scallops that have been soaked in a weight-enhancing preservative solution will not brown properly and will have an entirely different texture and taste.

1½ **pounds dry-pack sea scallops**

½ **teaspoon salt**

½ **teaspoon sugar**

½ **teaspoon dried basil**

½ **teaspoon dried thyme**

¼ **teaspoon garlic powder**

¼ **teaspoon onion powder**

2 **teaspoons vegetable oil or light olive oil**

Lemon wedges

1. If the scallops are damp or wet, pat dry with paper towels. To make the seasoning mix, in a small bowl, combine the salt, sugar, basil, thyme, garlic powder, and onion powder. Stir well.

2. In one or two large (preferably cast-iron) skillets, heat the oil over medium-high heat. Sprinkle the scallops very lightly on both sides with the seasoning mix. When the oil is hot, arrange the scallops in the pan in a single layer, without touching. Cook, adjusting the heat if necessary, until the bottoms are nicely browned and caramelized, 3 to 4 minutes. Turn with tongs and cook on the other side until the scallops are just firm to the touch and lightly browned on the bottom, another 2 to 4 minutes, depending on their size.

3. Serve with the lemon wedges.

4 servings

Thurston's Lobster Pound

Bernard, Maine

From Thurston's

CRAB LOUIS SPREAD (PAGE 30)
MUSSEL CHOWDER (PAGE 62)
BOILED LOBSTERS (PAGE 128)

Mike Radcliffe's great-grandfather Fred Thurston started a lobster wholesaling business back in 1946, and Fred and his grandson built the operation into one of the largest of its kind on Maine's Mount Desert Island. When Mike and his wife, Libby, took over in the early 1990s, they started the restaurant branch of the business, appreciating that this spot overlooking beautiful Bass Harbor, one of the last remaining working fishing harbors on this large island, could not be a more ideal

site from which to feed locals and summer visitors some of the freshest lobsters ever to hit the plate. Seventy lobster boats work from this harbor, and Thurston's buys lobsters from almost half of them. So, as you wait for your crustacean to cook, you sit on one of the twin-tiered, awning-shaded decks and observe the fascinating activity that surrounds a working dock. The menu is limited to what they do best: lobster, chosen from the tanks near the ordering window, and seawater-boiled outside in a propane-fired cooker. If you want steamer clams, mussels, or corn, they're added to the net bag so that everything picks up the sweet flavor of the water. (Some customers will only come late in the day, when the water has acquired maximum flavor.)

Homemade chowders (all aged for at least a day) rotate from scallop to haddock to mussel, and a simple but elegant lobster stew is made with the broth they get from boiling the lobster shells. The menu rounds out with seafood salad rolls (lobster and crab), burgers and dogs, and a lovely Crab Louis Spread made with sweet local crabmeat that makes a great appetizer. Desserts are three kinds of homemade pie, shortcakes, and Ben & Jerry's ice cream.

CLAMORING FOR A CLAMBAKE

It's called a "lobster bake" in Maine, but everywhere else in New England this ancient, atavistic method of cooking lobsters and other shellfish on the beach is known as a "clambake." The tradition is inherited directly from the Native Americans, who cooked all their food this way in their summer encampments up and down the New England coastline.

The basic technique involves digging a deep pit in the sand and lining it with rocks, upon which is built a driftwood or hardwood fire. When the fire burns down, the coals are raked away, and wet rockweed seaweed, which is laden with tiny sacs full of salt water, is layered over the white-hot rocks. The food is laid on the seaweed, and a heavy canvas tarpaulin is spread over all to seal in the heat. As the rockweed heats and releases water, the salty steam cooks the food, and when the tarp is lifted, the heavenly ocean-sweet, smoky aroma of steamed seafood perfumes the sea air.

Traditional clambake foods include lobsters, clams, corn, potatoes, and, anywhere near Rhode Island, with its large Portuguese population, spicy smoked sausage. Other ingredients vary from one locale to the next. Mussels, chicken, onions, frankfurters, sweet potatoes, crabs, whole fish, and eggs are sometimes added.

Constructing a genuine pit-in-the-sand clambake on a beach takes superb organizational skill and is at least an all-day affair. You need a group of hardworking family or friends — or, if it's being put on as a fund-raiser, as many clambakes are now, a diligent committee. Serving as the "bakemaster" is an honored position that must be earned by serving years of apprenticeship as a bakemaster's helper.

Backyard Clambake. A simplified backyard or kitchen version of a clambake involves a fraction of the work yet still produces one of the most extravagant-looking and downright delicious meals of summer. Sometimes dubbed a "New England shore dinner," the menu can include any or all the traditional elements, plus or minus dishes of your own choosing. Boil or steam the lobsters, clams or mussels, and corn in the kitchen, or on a gas grill, or use a camp-style setup in the backyard with a large pot set on a tripod and heated over a propane burner.

Public Clambake. But if you're not up to even the simplified version of hosting your own clambake and you are visiting the Maine coast, you can still participate in the drama and fun of a traditional New England clambake. Some organizations put them on as fund raisers, so look for announcements on notice boards or in local newspapers. If you're in the Boothbay Harbor area in the summer, check out the Cabbage Island Clambake. The Moore family has been staging these daily events on scenic Cabbage Island in Linekin Bay since 1956. Additional information is available at the Fisherman's Wharf Inn (see Resources, page 240).

BACKYARD CLAMBAKE MENU

Thurston's Crab Louis Spread
(page 30)

Creamy Cape Cod
Clam Chowder
(page 60)

Thurston's Boiled Lobsters
(page 128)

Tidal Falls' Garlicky Mussels
(page 129)

The Place's Roast Corn
(page 191)

Coffin Family Coleslaw
(page 195)

Cod End's Maine
Wild Blueberry Pie
(page 222)

Fried Maine Shrimp

Maine shrimp (also called *northern pink shrimp*) are fished out of the Gulf of Maine in the wintertime and are the only shrimp that New Englanders get in a truly fresh state. They are tiny and sweet — and they freeze well, so they can be savored in the summer at such places as Two Lights Lobster Shack in Cape Elizabeth, Maine, where they fry these popcorn-size morsels to perfection. Two Lights is famous for their Shrimp Boat, which consists of a hefty heap of the crispy shrimp, along with fabulous fries and pineapple-sweetened coleslaw.

Soybean oil for frying

¼   **pound shelled Maine shrimp**

1½ **cups breading mix**

Lemon wedges

Tartar sauce

1. Heat the oil over medium heat in a deep fryer or deep pot to 375°F. (See Note.)

2. The shrimp should be somewhat damp. If they are not, rinse them under cold water and shake off the excess water. Place the breading in a bowl. Add about half the shrimp to the breading and toss with your fingers so that each shrimp is well coated with the flour mixture. If the breading mixture begins to get clumpy, place the breaded shrimp in a large strainer and shake it to remove the excess flour.

3. Slide the shrimp into the hot oil and cook until they are golden brown and float, 1 to 2 minutes. Drain on paper towels. Repeat with the remaining shrimp.

4. Serve with lemon wedges and tartar sauce.

NOTE: You could also shallow-fry the shrimp in ½ to ¼ inch of oil. (See Frying Basics, page 146.)

2 servings

Grill-Roasted Lobster

The 25-foot hardwood-fired grill at The Place in Guilford, Connecticut, is loaded all summer with local bounty from land and sea, but nothing is more glorious than their grill-roasted lobsters, which are parboiled and then finished directly on the grill, where they pick up a hint of smoke and char. It requires nothing more than a daub of butter and a squirt of lemon to gild the beautiful crustacean. The only slightly tricky part is splitting the partially cooked lobsters, but if you use a large, heavy chef's knife and wear a pair of heavy-duty rubber gloves, you'll do fine.

4   live lobsters, about
    1¼ to 1½ pounds
    each

Salt and freshly ground
    black pepper

½   cup (1 stick) butter,
    melted, plus addi-
    tional for serving

Lemon wedges

1. Build a moderately hot hardwood or charcoal fire or preheat a gas grill.

2. Bring a large pot of water to the boil. Add about 1 tablespoon of salt. Plunge the lobsters into the boiling water, cover the pot, and return to the boil. Cook for 5 to 8 minutes, or until the lobsters are beginning to turn bright red. They should be about half cooked at this point. Drain. Place each lobster top-shell up on a cutting board and, using a large chef's knife, split lengthwise through the shell. Remove the intestinal vein. (The lobsters can be prepared 1 hour ahead to this point. Cool, cover, and refrigerate.)

3. Place the lobsters, cut-sides down, on the grill, and cook until the tail meat is firm and marked with stripes from the grill, about 5 minutes.

4. Brush liberally with melted butter and season with salt and pepper. Pass additional melted butter and lemon wedges at the table.

4 servings

Calvin's Theory of Evolution

"IT IS APPARENT TO SERIOUS SHELLFISH EATERS that in the great evolutionary scheme of things crustaceans developed shells to protect them from knives and forks."

— Calvin Trillin

Alice, Let's Eat

LOBSTER POUND PROTOCOL

Eat-in-the-rough lobster pounds are the ultimate in casual dining, so the dress code is nil. In fact, it's a good idea to deliberately dress down, since lobster cracking and eating and steamer slurping tends to be a messy process, and you wouldn't want to risk squirting lobster juice on your good silk blouse. Some additional guidelines:

- If you want beer or wine, call ahead. Many places don't have a license, but most will let you bring your own and will probably provide glasses and uncork your wine.

- You'll probably be eating at a picnic table (some are family-style), either in a screened pavilion or outdoors, so it's a good idea to pack some bug repellent. Hopefully you'll be overlooking a knockout water view, so it's nice to get there during the daylight hours in order to fully enjoy your surroundings.

- New England evenings can be chillier near the water, so carry a sweater or light jacket.

And then . . . tie on your plastic bib and begin the attack!

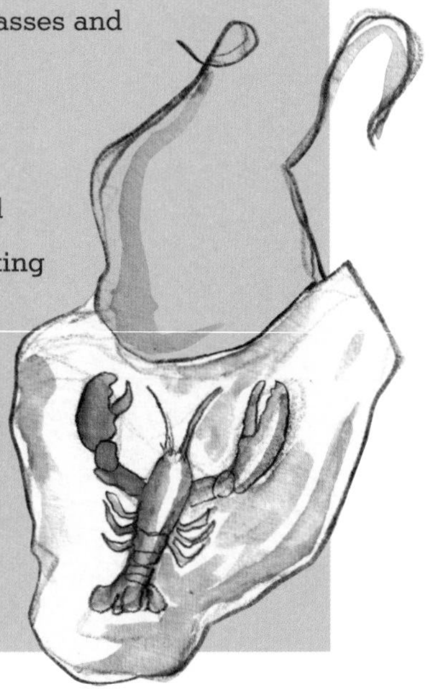

Two Lights Lobster Shack

Cape Elizabeth, Maine

From Two Lights

FRIED MAINE SHRIMP (PAGE 116)

OATMEAL PIE (PAGE 229)

"**E**njoy our famous dinners. Eat In or Take Out. Come as you are. Bring the Whole Family." This has been the Porch and Leadbetter families' motto since they opened Two Lights (so named because it sits below a lighthouse and next to a foghorn) in 1968. The setting is simply spectacular, for the restaurant is perched on a rocky headland right on the Atlantic at the entrance to Portland Harbor. All food is ordered from their take-out window and line, but you then have the choice of eating oceanside at one of the 30 or so picnic tables or inside, in the cheery, varnished wood dining room. The menu runs the gamut from complete seawater-steamed lobster dinners and heaping fisherman's plates, to simply wonderful home-made clam chowder and lobster stew, to the classic clam shack offerings of fried sea-food "boats" (their Maine shrimp boat is

particularly notable), lobster and crabmeat rolls, hamburgers, hot dogs, and veggie burgers. All seafood is local and is purchased, if possible, from other family-run businesses. Founder Jim Leadbetter, who now runs the adjoining made-in-Maine gift shop, comes from a long line of bakers, and, in fact, he himself baked for the restaurant until he was 80 years old! This family tradition is being carried on by his grandson, who now makes all Two Lights' desserts, including éclairs, apple cream turnovers, raisin bread pudding, mini blueberry pies, and the unusual and scrumptious Oatmeal Pie.

THE BEST WAY TO EAT A LOBSTER

1. Twist off the two large claws where they meet the body. Separate the pincer claws from the knuckles. Using a nutcracker, crack the claws and the knuckles. The claw meat is easy to get at; sometimes you have to poke out the knuckle meat with a lobster pick or your little finger.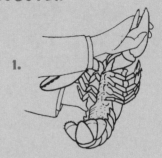

2. For the tail, grasp the lobster with one hand on the body and one hand on the tail and twist to break in two. Expect a gush of liquid on your plate, which you can drain into the shell debris bowl on the table.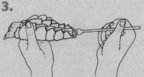

Remove the flippers at the end and pull each one through your teeth like an artichoke leaf.

3. Then if the tail hasn't been split, poke the tail meat out with a fork (if the lobster is hard-shell) or your finger (if it's soft-shell). Split the tail meat lengthwise, and remove and discard the black vein running down the center. Dip the meat into melted butter and eat.

4. Tucked away deep in the body is the soft green tomalley (sometimes referred to as the liver), and, if the lobster is female, the bright pink roe, or coral, reached by separating the shell of the body from the underside. Some consider these morsels, the rich-tasting tomalley in particular, to be the most prized lobster parts of all.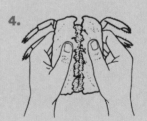

For the persistent person, there are still the small legs, again best eaten by pulling through your teeth to extract the meat. There are also small nuggets of meat in the joints where the legs meet the body.

Lazy Man's Lobster

When I asked Jane Patten, one of the cooks at Shaw's Fish and Lobster Wharf in New Harbor, Maine, to name their most popular menu item, she replied, "Lazy Man's Lobster, for sure." And why not? All the work is done for you, so all you have to do is sit back on the deck and feast on chunks of succulent, freshly picked lobster meat that has been drizzled with melted butter and finished with a dusting of rosy paprika.

4   **live lobsters, about 1½ pounds each**

½   **cup (1 stick) butter**

Salt and freshly ground black pepper

Paprika

Lemon wedges

1. Bring a large pot of salted water to the boil. Boil or steam the lobsters in or over the water until the shells turn bright red and the tail meat is firm and opaque when checked, about 15 minutes. Drain. When the lobsters are cool enough to handle, crack the claws and tail, extract the meat, and cut it into chunks no smaller than ¾ inch. Divide the lobster meat among four gratin dishes. (The dishes can be prepared ahead and refrigerated. Reheat for a few minutes on low power in a microwave before finishing.)

2. In a medium saucepan, melt the butter slowly over low heat. Do not let it bubble.

3. Pour the melted butter over the warm lobster. Season with salt and pepper and sprinkle with paprika. Serve with lemon wedges on the side.

4 servings

A PEARL IN MANHATTAN

Pearl Oyster Bar is like a small shard of Down East essence transported intact and grafted onto Manhattan island — but with the addition of such civilized New York niceties as a sophisticated, well-chosen wine list, hot jazz snapping happily out of the sound system, and a hip, actorish waitstaff to ferry the fabulous food. In the mid-1990s, chef/owner Rebecca Charles, who spent childhood summers in Maine and then cooked at a high-end inn in Kennebunkport for several years, noted the absence in the city of first-rate, unpretentious restaurants showcasing New England's renowned seafood, and she responded by opening the Pearl in 1997. At lunch you can get a bowl of decadently rich, creamy chowder studded with bits of smoky bacon, or a lobster roll as good as any you'd order from a Down East take-out window — chunks of sweet lobster bound with just enough mayonnaise, heaped on a butter-grilled hot dog bun, and garnished with a lettuce frill. Fresh-shucked clams and oysters on the half shell, salt-fried shrimp, fried oysters returned to their shell nestling atop a pool of homemade tartar sauce, half a steamed, chilled Maine lobster, garlicky herb-steamed mussels, and a market fish sandwich are some of the other lunch offerings.

"At dinner," Rebecca says, "we really show 'em we know how to cook." Besides most of the lunch menu items, there are at least half a dozen daily blackboard specials. A spectacular New England bouillabaisse is always on the menu, there's a whole grilled garlic-and-herb-stuffed fish nightly, and lobster is served boiled or grilled, with a side of golden corn pudding. Desserts are well-made versions of Yankee favorites: seasonal pies (berry and cream), cobblers, sundaes, and a simply superb maple crème brûlée.

PEARL

Rebecca Charles

18 Cornelia Street

NYC, NY 10014

Tel: 212 • 691 • 8211

Soft-Shell Crabs Provençale

Although soft-shell crabs aren't native to New England (most come from the warmer waters of the Chesapeake Bay), chef Bob Sader of the Seahorse Tavern in Noank, Connecticut, makes a point of putting them on his menu every April and May as a harbinger of spring. He makes them several ways — deep-fried as a po' boy sandwich, blackened Cajun-style — but his personal favorite is this simple pan sauté topped with a garlicky tomato-wine sauce flecked with fresh basil. You might take a cue from the Seahorse and serve the crabs with mashed potatoes or pasta, along with fresh asparagus or broccolini on the side.

8   small soft-shell crabs (about 4 ounces each), cleaned (see Note)

1   cup all-purpose flour

1   teaspoon salt, plus additional for sauce

½   teaspoon freshly ground black pepper, plus additional for sauce

4   tablespoons butter, plus 2 tablespoons

2   teaspoons finely chopped garlic

1   cup dry white wine

2   tomatoes, seeded and finely chopped

8   fresh basil leaves, slivered

1. Pat the crabs dry with paper towels. Combine the flour, salt, and pepper on a plate. Dredge the crabs in the seasoned flour, shaking off the excess.

2. Divide the 4 tablespoons butter between two large skillets and set over medium heat. Add the crabs and cook over medium to medium-high heat until nicely browned on both sides, about 10 minutes total. Remove to a platter and tent with foil to keep warm.

3. Use just one of the skillets to make the sauce. Discard the butter in it if it's burned and add the remaining 2 tablespoons of butter to the pan. Add the garlic and cook over medium heat for 1 minute. Add the wine, increase the heat to high, and boil until the wine reduces by about half, about 3 minutes. Add the tomatoes and basil and cook, uncovered, for about 5 minutes, until the sauce is lightly thickened. Season with salt and pepper to taste.

4. Spoon the sauce over the crabs and serve.

NOTE: Purchase crabs live from the fish market, or frozen. If the crabs are live, ask the fish market to clean them for you.

4 servings

Champlin's Seafood

Narragansett, Rhode Island

Champlin's has been a restaurant and retail seafood market on this site on the Block Island ferry slip in the Port of Galilee for more than 80 years. It started as a little shack in the 1920s. After the whole shoreline was destroyed by mid-twentieth-century hurricanes, Champlin's was rebuilt as an upstairs deck. More wings and decks were tacked on over the years, so that now the place sprawls around in a charmingly idiosyncratic manner.

Galilee Harbor is home of Rhode Island's largest fishing fleet, and Champlin's pays tribute to that fact — not only by serving up that just-delivered fish, but also by honoring the men who catch it by decorating the walls with photographs of fishermen and with a roll call of local fishing boats. The service is strictly "in the rough": You place your order at a window, pick it up after your number is called, and carry your food to one of the indoor or outside tables.

Many of Champlin's dishes are the kind of simple, unadorned fare for which New England seafood

From Champlin's

SNAIL SALAD (PAGE 8)

RHODE ISLAND RED CLAM CHOWDER (PAGE 55)

FRIED CALAMARI WITH PICKLED PEPPERS (PAGE 110)

houses are famous, but some menu items show off more than a hint of that unique Rhode Island flair. Fried clams, scallop rolls, fish and chips, and charbroiled swordfish coexist on their extensive menu with fish cakes and a Rhode Island red chowder that contains a bit of a peppery kick. Their scrumptious, golden, deep-fried rings of calamari are garnished with pickled hot pepper rings.

In addition to such traditional sides as onion rings, corn on the cob, and coleslaw, Champlin's offers snail salad, a deliciously garlicky Rhode Island specialty that tastes a lot better than it might sound. No dessert is served, but you can stop in for an ice cream cone in the shop downstairs before going next door to buy some seafood for tomorrow night's supper from Champlin's retail fish market.

Boiled Lobsters

There is truly no more magnificent feast than a lobster dinner, whether it's eaten at a lobster pound picnic table or on your very own deck. At Thurston's Lobster Pound in Bernard, Maine, on Mount Desert Island, you choose your lobsters from the tanks near the order window, and then they're boiled in clean seawater in a large propane-fired cooker. To replicate at home, just be sure to add enough salt to the water to create the right balance of ocean-briny flavor. A mere swipe through melted butter, a squirt of lemon — and that's all anyone needs. Heaven!

2 to 3 tablespoons salt

4   live lobsters, about 1½ pounds each

½   cup (1 stick) melted butter

Lemon wedges

1. Fill a large stockpot about half full of water (see Note). Add the salt and bring to a boil.

2. When the water has come to a rolling boil, plunge the lobsters headfirst into the pot. Clamp the lid back on tightly and return the water to a boil over high heat. Reduce the heat to medium and cook the lobsters for 12 to 18 minutes (hard-shell lobsters will take the longer time), until the shells turn bright red and the tail meat is firm and opaque when checked.

3. Lift the lobsters out of the water with tongs and drain in a colander. Place underside up on a work surface and, grasping firmly, split the tails lengthwise with a large knife. Drain off the excess liquid. Serve with melted butter and lemon wedges.

NOTE: Or you can steam in about 2 inches of water with about a tablespoon of salt.

4 servings

HUMANE LOBSTER COOKING

Lobsters must be kept alive until they are cooked because their flesh begins to deteriorate soon after they die or are killed. Some experts recommend numbing the lobsters first by placing them in the freezer for about 10 minutes before cooking.

Garlicky Mussels

There are several reasons why the mussels at Tidal Falls Lobster Restaurant in Hancock, Maine, taste superb. They harvest wild mussels from the bay near the restaurant, and they're always fresh and clean, due to the constant sweep of water in the bay. Then, once harvested, the mussels live in the same seawater tank with Tidal Falls' lobsters. Finally, the mussels are steamed over some of that fresh, clean, tidal seawater. But let's not forget the garlic butter either — a non-Maine-like tradition begun by the French former owner of Tidal Falls and now so popular in the area that they wouldn't dream of ever changing it! Be sure to add a basket of crusty French bread for sopping up all those garlicky juices.

5   **large garlic cloves**

½   **pound (2 sticks) butter**

2   **teaspoons salt**

6   **pounds live mussels, rinsed**

1. Peel the garlic and put through a garlic press or finely mince with a chef's knife. In a saucepan, melt the butter over low heat. Add the garlic and cook over very low heat for 5 minutes. Remove from the heat and set aside, covered, for at least 1 hour. (Garlic butter can be refrigerated for up to 3 days. Reheat gently.)

2. In a large stockpot, bring about 1 inch of water to a boil. Add the salt. Add the mussels, cover the pot, and bring to the boil. Reduce the heat to medium and steam until the mussel shells open, 5 to 10 minutes, depending on their size and the size of the pot. Use a slotted spoon to transfer the mussels to a large platter; discard any that do not open.

3. Meanwhile, reheat the garlic butter over low heat. Pour the warm garlic butter over the hot mussels, and serve.

6 servings

and...

CHAPTER 6

Fish Fried and Broiled, and One Great Grilled Chicken

One of the myriad virtues of classic New England clam shacks, lobster pounds, and chowder houses is that the best ones follow the "stick with what you know" credo — and when you do that, you can hardly ever go wrong. With finfish, what they know best is, of course, local. Local in Connecticut and Massachusetts means haddock and cod, flounder and bluefish. In Rhode Island, add swordfish and striped bass and halibut to the list. New Hampshire is lucky enough to get a good winter run of ocean smelts. And in Maine, lesser-known pollack, hake, and cusk join the roll call. So, when you get your hands on freshly caught, local fish, what's the best way to treat it? Cook it simply, and that means broiling, grilling, and baking, with the occasional indulgence in deep-frying or splurge on a rich seafood stuffing. And should you ever tire of the all-seafood-all-the-time diet, consider building a hardwood fire in the grill and cooking yourself up some barbecued chicken breasts à la The Place in Guilford, Connecticut.

Broiled Flounder

There's nothing quite as sweet or delicate as a newly caught flounder, and since tons of it arrive at the Narragansett, Rhode Island, fishing pier every week, Aunt Carrie's restaurant has a steady supply of the very freshest of the fresh. And that's the only secret, along with using this simple cooking technique: broiling, but with a little steam to keep the flesh from drying out. It's the perfect way to treat a really fresh flounder or any other flatfish.

4 to 8 flounder fillets (depending on size), about 1½ pounds total

Salt and freshly ground black pepper

4 tablespoons butter, melted

Paprika, optional

Lemon wedges

1. Preheat the broiler. Position an oven rack about 6 inches from the heat source. Lightly butter a rimmed baking sheet or large roasting pan.

2. Arrange fish in a single layer in the pan. Season very lightly with salt and pepper. Pour water into the pan to cover the bottom but not the fish. Drizzle with the melted butter.

3. Place under the preheated broiler and cook until the fish is pale golden brown on top and cooked through in its thickest part, 5 to 7 minutes, depending on the thickness of the fish.

4. Remove from the oven and carefully pour the water out of the pan. Using a wide spatula, carefully transfer the fish directly to serving plates.

5. Sprinkle with paprika if desired and serve with lemon wedges.

4 servings

Baked Stuffed Haddock

Baked Stuffed Haddock is a regular and ever-popular menu item at BG's Boat House in Portsmouth, New Hampshire, but chef Jeff Graves also uses this rich, deliciously buttery seafood stuffing for sole, jumbo shrimp, and lobster. This makes an impressive and elegant party dish.

3   **tablespoons butter**

3   **tablespoons olive oil**

1   **small onion, chopped**

½   **a small zucchini, unpeeled and chopped**

½   **cup chopped fresh mushrooms**

½   **pound sea scallops, chopped**

½   **pound small ("salad size") peeled and deveined shrimp (if using larger shrimp, coarsely chop)**

1½   **teaspoons Old Bay or other seafood seasoning blend**

1½   **cups crushed Ritz cracker crumbs (about 1¼ sleeves of crackers)**

Salt and freshly ground black pepper

8   **thin haddock or other whitefish fillets, about 2 pounds total**

2   **tablespoons butter, melted**

Lemon wedges

1. In a large skillet, heat the butter and oil. Add the onion, zucchini, and mushrooms. Cook over medium-high heat, stirring often, until the vegetables are softened and lightly browned, about 6 minutes. Add the scallops, shrimp, and Old Bay seasoning and cook, stirring, until the seafood is just cooked through, 3 to 4 minutes. Remove from the heat.

2. Add the Ritz cracker crumbs, and season to taste with salt and pepper. (The stuffing can be made up to 1 day ahead and refrigerated. Bring to room temperature or take the chill off in the microwave before stuffing the fish.)

3. Preheat the oven to 400°F. Brush individual gratin dishes or a large glass baking dish generously with melted butter.

4. Season the fish fillets on both sides with salt and pepper. Place a fillet in each gratin dish, or arrange four of the fillets in the baking dish. Cover with stuffing, pressing it in to make an even layer, and top with the remaining fillets. If some of the seafood stuffing spills out into the dish, that's fine. Brush the fish with melted butter.

5. Bake in the preheated oven until the fish is opaque in its thickest part and the stuffing is heated through, 20 to 30 minutes, depending on the thickness of the fish. Garnish with lemon wedges for squeezing over the fish.

4 servings

BG's Boat House Restaurant

Portsmouth, New Hampshire

From BG's Boat House

PORTSMOUTH SEAFOOD CHOWDER (PAGE 52)
BAKED STUFFED HADDOCK (PAGE 133)
FRIED SMELTS (PAGE 150)

"**W**elcome to BG's Boat House Restaurant," reads the menu. "Our food is always cooked to order. We have outdoor dining by our marina on 2 decks with a sidle-up bar. Our indoor dining room is air-conditioned or heated depending on New England weather. A customer docking space is available in our marina and rafting is permitted. Please enjoy our cozy restaurant, traditional food, and water view." You can't help enjoying yourself at this delightful, down-to-earth, full-service restaurant that serves up a complete roster of traditional New England food at its best. BG's has been doing business for 30 years, and they

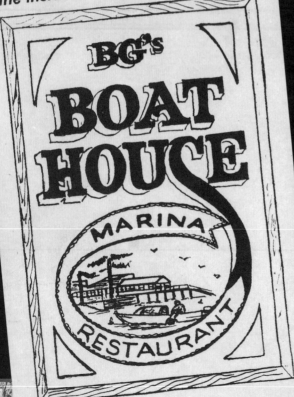

Dine inside or outside, on the water at

BG's BOAT HOUSE MARINA RESTAURANT

All Items Available For Take-Out 431-1074

seem to have the formula down to a science — and a simple yet foolproof formula it is. All the seafood is hand-chosen daily (as much from local sources as possible), and every individually cooked order arrives at the table piping hot and super fresh — and that's all in addition to seating on decks and with pretty views of water and boats. The fact that the restaurant is also a marina is a big plus for boaters. The extensive menu includes fabulous lobster dishes of all kinds and the full spectrum of various other New England seafood specialties, baked, broiled, steamed, grilled, and fried. Saltwater smelts are a favorite, as is the homemade seafood chowder, broiled scallops, fried clam basket (whole-belly clams or strips), and superb seafood-stuffed haddock. BG's also offers plenty of choices for the non-fish-eater.

Broiled Bluefish Dijonnaise

Bluefish is not a regular menu item at Land Ho! in Orleans, Massachusetts — the catch is too unpredictable, and bluefish is good only when it's really fresh — but on those propitious days when the boat brings bluefish in, they run it as a special, adding it to the ever-changing chalkboard that hangs above the bar. One of the chef's most popular treatments is simply to broil the succulent fish and serve it with a quickly made dijonnaise sauce, with sides of homemade mashed potatoes and fresh asparagus.

Dijonnaise Sauce

1	cup mayonnaise
2	tablespoons Dijon mustard, preferably coarse-ground
1	tablespoon lemon juice
¼	teaspoon salt
¼	teaspoon white pepper
1½	tablespoons chopped fresh dill

Fish

4	skinless bluefish fillets, 6 to 8 ounces each
2	tablespoons butter
	Salt and freshly ground black pepper
⅓	cup dry white wine

1. For the sauce, whisk together the mayonnaise, mustard, lemon juice, salt, and pepper. Stir in the dill. (The sauce may be refrigerated for up to 2 days; return to room temperature before serving.)

2. Preheat the broiler with a rack 4 to 5 inches from the element. Oil the broiler pan.

3. Arrange the bluefish in the prepared pan. Cut the butter into small pieces, distribute it over the top of the fish, and season with salt and pepper. Pour the wine around the fish.

4. Broil 4 to 5 inches from the element, until the top is flecked with golden brown and the fish is opaque in its thickest part, 4 to 8 minutes, depending on the thickness of the fish.

5. Transfer to serving plates and pass the mustard sauce to spoon over the fish.

4 servings

Keep It Simple

"WE'VE ALL LEARNED A LOT from Alice Waters [California restaurateur and fresh food guru]. The concept of simplicity — using great raw ingredients, treated simply and with respect — applies to humble little places like mine as well as to fancy, expensive restaurants."

— Dave Blaney
Sea Swirl

PORTUGUESE IN NEW ENGLAND

In the early nineteenth century, New England whaling captains, hearing of the legendary reputation of the Portuguese as expert seamen, departed New England ports intending to fill in the balance of their crew with Portuguese recruits, particularly from the Azores. After traveling around the globe in pursuit of whales, a good many of these Portuguese sailors collected their wages back in New Bedford and other New England whaling ports and settled down there to raise families. Others immigrated to other seaport towns in Rhode Island and Massachusetts, seeking to market their well-honed sea-related skills in the rapidly growing fishing industry in the New World. Of course, they brought their food — a repertoire of fantastic seafood dishes, many of which are highly seasoned with garlic and peppers and other spices; spicy linguiça and chourico sausages; and sweet breads, eggy tarts, and numerous other confections.

Roasted Striped Bass with Vegetable Garnish

When the stripers are running, Chopmist Charlie's owner Chuck Masso enjoys fishing for them himself in Narragansett Bay. Meaty striped bass takes particularly well to high-heat oven roasting, and this treatment, with the fish enhanced by an herb-infused marinade and a shower of fresh vegetables, often appears as a menu special at his Jamestown, Rhode Island, restaurant during striper season in summer. Chopmist is so famous for its striped bass that Chuck Masso recently started selling t-shirts imprinted with the testimonial, "Best Piece of Bass I Ever Had!"

⅓   cup olive oil

3   tablespoons lemon juice

1   tablespoon minced garlic

¼   cup slivered fresh basil, plus sprigs for garnish

1   teaspoon salt

½   teaspoon freshly ground black pepper

4   skinless, boneless striped bass fillets, about 8 ounces each

1   cup cherry tomatoes, halved

1   medium-sized onion, thinly sliced

¼   cup thinly sliced celery

Lemon wedges

1. In a large shallow dish, whisk together the oil, lemon juice, garlic, slivered basil, salt, and pepper. Add the fish, turn to coat with the marinade, cover, and refrigerate for at least 2 hours or overnight.

2. Preheat the oven to 425°F. Lift the fillets out of the marinade and arrange in a single layer in a large baking dish. Scatter the tomatoes, onions, and celery over and around the fish, and pour the rest of the marinade over the top.

3. Bake, uncovered, in the preheated oven until the fish is no longer translucent in its thickest part and the vegetables are softened, 10 to 20 minutes, depending on the thickness of the fish. (To caramelize and lightly brown the vegetables, run under a broiler for about 1 minute.)

4. Garnish with basil sprigs and serve accompanied by lemon wedges.

4 servings

Fresh Salmon Fish and Chips

Five Islands fish and chips made with fresh salmon just might be the most succulent version of this meal you've ever encountered. They take a salmon steak, cut it in chunks, bread it very lightly, and fry it in impeccably fresh oil. The salmon emerges lightly crusted on the outside and pink and incredibly moist within. It's served up with crisp crinkle cut fries, a wedge of lemon, and one of Five Islands three special homemade sauces (see Note).

Vegetable oil for deep frying

1 pound frozen crinkle cut French fries

Salt

4 boneless salmon steaks, 4 to 5 ounces each, cut into 2½- to 3-inch chunks

1½ cups breading mix

Lemon wedges

Tartar sauce or other Five Islands–style sauce (see Note)

1. Heat 2 inches of oil in a large skillet or fill a deep fryer with oil and heat to 350°F.

2. Cook the fries in the oil until golden and crisp, 3 to 5 minutes. Drain on paper towels and sprinkle with salt. (Or do the potatoes in the oven according to package directions.)

3. Dredge the salmon in the breading mix, shaking off the excess. Slide into the hot oil and cook until golden brown and the fish tests done, 2 to 3 minutes.

4. Serve the salmon with the fries, a lemon wedge, and a bowl of sauce for dipping.

NOTE: To create a facsimile of Five Islands Tartar sauce, stir some capers, chopped dill, and scallions into bottled mayonnaise. Their Mustard Dill sauce starts with homemade mayonnaise and is flavored with mustard and chopped dill; the Cilantro Mayo also uses a homemade base and is seasoned with fresh cilantro, garlic, and jalapeño peppers.

4 servings

Baked Scrod with Lemon-Garlic Crumbs

This is what my friend Susan Maloney (intrepid seeker of great clam shacks, and to whom this book is dedicated) always eats at Quito's in Bristol, Rhode Island — after perhaps polishing off a cup of chowder or sharing an order of littlenecks in garlic and oil. This simple preparation of crumb-topped baked fish is almost totally dependent on the quality of the seafood — and because there's also a retail fish market on the premises you can always count on absolute freshness at Quito's.

2	pounds fresh scrod, cod, or haddock
12	tablespoons (1½ sticks) butter
½	cup cream sherry
Juice of 1 lemon	
3	cups finely crushed Ritz cracker crumbs (2 sleeves)
3	tablespoon chopped parsley
1	tablespoon chopped garlic
½	teaspoon salt
¼	teaspoon black pepper
¼	teaspoon cayenne pepper
Lemon wedges	

1. Preheat the oven to 375°F. Generously butter a baking dish large enough to hold fish in a single layer and arrange fish in dish.

2. In a medium saucepan combine the butter, sherry, and lemon juice and cook over medium heat until butter melts.

3. In a bowl, toss the cracker crumbs with the parsley, garlic, salt, pepper, and cayenne. Add the melted butter mixture and mix well. Sprinkle the crumbs thickly over the fish.

4. Bake in the preheated oven for 35 to 45 minutes until fish tests done and the crumbs are golden brown. Serve with lemon wedges.

4 to 6 servings

Five Islands Lobster Company

Georgetown, Maine

From Five Islands

JENNY'S SPECIAL SANDWICH (PAGE 102)

FRESH SALMON FISH AND CHIPS (PAGE 140)

CRUSTY CRACKER-DREDGED ONION RINGS (PAGE 199)

For sheer Maine beauty — and there's lots of it on this coast — Five Islands Lobster Company's location and view are unsurpassed. Situated on a working lobster wharf, the restaurant consists of three buildings — the red Lobster Company shack, where you pick out your "bug" and have it steamed, the Love Nest Grill next door (named because allegedly fishermen held trysts upstairs here before shipping out on long voyages), where you can get something fried or grilled, and a building that houses Annabelle's Ice Cream *and* a bait shed. Lobster boats ply the spectacularly scenic harbor, expertly maneuvering around fancy pleasure craft, and then bring their catch into the dock to be weighed and sold. Fishermen and teenage summer employees enjoy an easy camaraderie, and the banter and jokes fly.

After you've become sated with beauty, place your order at one of the windows and stake out a claim at a picnic table on the wharf. (There is no indoor seating here.)

All the food is superb. The steamed lobsters — often a soft-shell or "shedder," which is easier to tear into than a hard-shell — are right from the deep, cold waters off this dock. All the fried seafood is prepared with extreme care — lightly breaded and fried in clean canola oil that is filtered every day and changed frequently. The clams are big bellied and sweet, the scallops tender, the salmon fish and chips succulent, and the Jenny Special Sandwich (grilled fresh-caught haddock topped with a crab cake and piled into a bun), unique and utterly decadent. And if you're sated with seafood, there are plenty of nonfish menu options, including burgers, hot dogs, and chicken wraps.

The entire Five Islands package — scenery, food, and people — is one that is truly emblematic of Maine.

HOW TO CLEAN AND FILLET FISH

To clean fish:

1. Use heavy scissors to cut off the fins.

2. Unless you are skinning the fish later, remove the scales with a special scaling tool or the back of a large knife, working from tail to head. Since the scales will scatter around, this procedure is best done outside.

3. Cut a slit along the length of the fish's belly. Pull out and discard the innards.

4. Rinse the fish.

Proceed with filleting or cutting into steaks. (Or, if serving the fish whole or split, as in the Tip For Tops'n Broiled Mackerel recipe, page 153, use scissors to cut out the gills near the head and, if desired, remove the head and tail.)

To fillet round fish (including haddock and bluefish):

1. Cut down to the backbone just behind the gills. Do not remove the head. Turn the knife toward the tail and cut to the tail, holding the knife parallel and close to the backbone.

2. To detach the fillet from the head, cut behind the gills.

3. Repeat on the other side.

4. Trim the rib bones from the sides of each of the two fillets with a flexible knife.

To fillet flatfish (including flounder):

1. Place the fish dark-skin-side up and cut along the backbone from head to tail.

2. Using a flexible knife, hold the knife against the rib bones and cut sideways to the edge of the fish and remove the fillet completely.

3. Remove the second fillet from this side using the same procedure.

4. Turn the fish over and remove the two fillets from the underside.

Fried Flounder

At The Bite in Menemsha on Martha's Vineyard, they make their fish and chips with flounder that gets delivered to their door fresh from the boat every day. They deep-fry it in clean vegetable oil, until the batter-and-crumb crust enveloping it is all crusty and golden. Just add some fries or chips and a bowl of coleslaw to re-create one of the best meals of summer. At home, you might find it easier to choose the shallow-fry cooking option.

Vegetable oil for frying

1½ cups breading mix

1¼ to 1½ cups water

1½ cups fine dry unsea-
soned breadcrumbs

2   pounds flounder
fillets

Lemon wedges or malt or
white wine vinegar

Tartar sauce

1. Heat the oil over medium heat in a deep fryer or heavy, deep pot to 350°F (see Note).

2. In a wide bowl, whisk the breading mix with 1¼ cups of the water. It should be a thin batter, about the consistency of buttermilk. Whisk in the remaining water, if necessary. Spread the breadcrumbs out in a wide, shallow dish.

3. Dip each piece of flounder into the batter and let the excess drip off. Dredge in the breadcrumbs, rolling to coat lightly but evenly. Slide into the hot oil and fry, turning once, until golden brown outside and opaque within, 2 to 4 minutes. Drain on paper towels. You will need to do this in two or three batches, depending on the size of your fryer.

4. Serve with lemon wedges or vinegar and tartar sauce.

NOTE: You could shallow-fry the fish in ½ to ¾ inch of oil (see Frying Basics, page 146).

4 servings

FRYING BASICS

Deep-frying. True deep-frying can be done on top of the stove in a large, deep pot or in an electric fryer equipped with a basket and a built-in thermostat.

The most suitable fats for home deep-frying are lard, hydrogenated solid white shortening, and liquid vegetable oil, such as canola, soybean, or peanut oil. Many restaurants use M/V, a meat/vegetable fat that is available only commercially. Lard imparts a mildly nutty flavor; the other fats are neutrally flavored. Olive oil, margarine, and butter are not good for deep-frying because of their low smoking point. (Recipes in this book specify the fat preference of each restaurant. Each chef chooses on the basis of flavor, availability, and cost. For purposes of the home cook, all the above-mentioned fats and oils are more or less interchangeable.)

Regardless of the type of fat you choose, follow these guidelines to deep-fry successfully at home:

- Use clean oil each time you fry.
- Fill the deep-fryer no more than about half full of fat.
- Melt or heat the fat over medium heat.
- Most restaurants fry when the fat is about 365°F. (Individual recipes specify different frying times used in a particular establishment.) Test the temperature with a deep-fry thermometer, or drop a 1-inch cube of bread into the oil and count to 60; if the bread browns in 1 minute, the oil should be about 365°F.

- Do not crowd the pan; fat should circulate freely around the food. Fry in batches if necessary.
- If the pan is not equipped with a basket, use a slotted spoon or tongs to remove food.
- Drain on paper towels.

Shallow-frying. Some foods that are deep-fried commercially can be "shallow-fried" by the home cook. Shallow-frying is safer because you are not dealing with a large quantity of hot oil. It is also less wasteful of oil.

Shallow-frying is done in about ¾ inch of oil in a cast-iron skillet or pot. Use the cube of bread technique described above to make sure the oil has reached the correct temperature.

Shallow-frying is especially suitable for cooking smaller batches of battered or breaded fried food. Individual recipes in this book specify when shallow-frying is a good option.

To Bread or Batter? When a recipe calls for breading mix, look for a product (usually shelved with Shake and Bake and other coating mixes) that calls itself "breading mix" or "fry mix" and lists such ingredients as corn flour, all-purpose flour, whey, salt, and sometimes baking powder. Usually "batter mix" calls for adding water or other liquid,  but often liquid can simply be added to breading mix, so in reality the two types of products are more or less interchangeable.

When you are breading, you might follow the advice of Pat Henderson, owner of Captain Frosty's on Cape Cod, who says hand-breading seafood requires care: "You really need to have people who care about what they're doing. If the cook is not paying attention — if they're not carefully shaking off all the excess breading mix, for instance — you're going to get an overly breaded product. You won't taste the seafood."

The Place

Guilford, Connecticut

From The Place

ROAST CLAMS (PAGE 35)
GRILL-ROASTED LOBSTER (PAGE 117)
ROAST BLUEFISH (PAGE 152)
WOOD-GRILLED BARBECUED CHICKEN (PAGE 156)
ROAST CORN (PAGE 191)

Idiosyncratic, loaded with charm, wonderfully unique — you've never been any place quite like The Place. Located right smack on Route 1 in Guilford, The Place is an oasis of quirky individualism (and fabulous food) in a franchised world. You smell the wood smoke wafting from the 25-foot grill before you see The Place. Constructed by local brothers/owners Gary and Vaughn Knowles when they bought The Place in the early 1970s, the grill is fired by hickory and oak only — and this magnificent structure is where *all* the cooking happens. Clams, chicken, fish, lobster, steaks, and corn on the cob are grilled, mussels and clams are steamed in pots over the fire, and everything picks up whispers or shouts of smoky flavor. The grill cooks (most wearing

shorts and rubber boots) expertly move food up and down the line as if they were choreographed, and as you sit on tree stumps at picnic tables under their red and white canopy watching the never-ending floor show, you feel like you're at a nonstop party. Since the menu is limited, "guests" are invited to bring their own extras, such as chips and salads, and to furnish their own tablecloths and pillows to cushion the "rump on the stump."

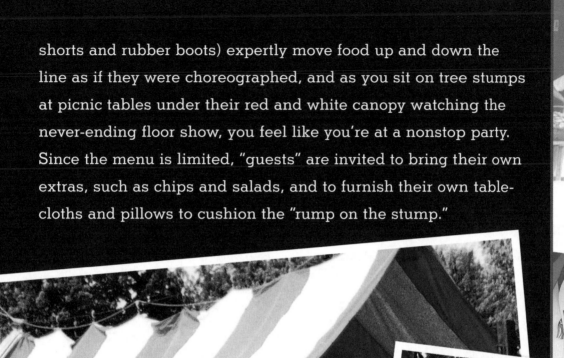

Fried Smelts

When I saw smelts listed as a menu special on my first trip to BG's Boat House in Portsmouth, New Hampshire, my instinct told me that this place was potentially book-worthy. In the cause of research, I had planned to eat just a few little smelts, but by the time I'd put away an entire order of these sublimely crunchy, perfectly fried morsels, my taste buds had convinced me that BG's was a definite keeper. (And this is after eating the seafood chowder and the clam roll!) Chef Jeff Graves can get these tiny fish fresh out of local waters during a short winter season, but frozen saltwater smelts are an excellent substitute.

Vegetable oil for frying

2   cups milk

2   cups breading mix

2   pounds dressed smelts

Lemon wedges

Tartar sauce

1. Heat the oil in a deep fryer or in a heavy, deep pot to 375°F. (See Note.)

2. Pour the milk into a large, wide bowl and put the breading mix in a similar bowl. Dip about one-third of the smelts (depending on the size of your fryer) into the milk wash and then into the breading mix; shake off the excess. You can place the breaded fish in a large strainer and shake it to remove the excess breading.

3. Slide the fish into the hot oil and cook until deep golden brown on all sides, about 3 minutes. Remove with a slotted spoon and drain on paper towels. Repeat with remaining fish. (The cooked fish can be kept warm in a slow oven for about 15 minutes.)

4. Serve with lemon wedges and tartar sauce.

NOTE: If making only a small batch, you could shallow-fry the fish in ½ to ¾ inch of oil. (See Frying Basics, page 146.)

6 to 8 first-course servings;
4 main-course servings

Skillet-Fried Haddock

At J's Oyster Bar in Portland, Maine, the menu always lists "Fish of the Day," and that fish is always haddock. And why not? Haddock is always available and always super fresh in this part of Maine. Buttery Ritz cracker crumbs form the perfectly delicious (and very New England–style) breading.

4   large pieces haddock fillet, 6 to 8 ounces each

2   eggs, lightly beaten with 2 tablespoons water

1½ cups crushed Ritz cracker crumbs (about one 4-ounce sleeve of crackers)

6   tablespoons butter

2   tablespoons vegetable oil

Lemon wedges

Parsley sprigs

1. Dip the fish in the egg wash and let the excess drip off. Dredge in the cracker crumbs, patting them on to the fish so that they adhere evenly.

2. Heat the butter and oil over medium-high heat in a very large (preferably cast-iron) frying pan. Add the fish to the pan (do not crowd — cook in two batches, if necessary), and cook, turning once, until the crumbs are deep golden brown and the flesh is opaque, about 8 minutes total. Regulate the heat so that the crumbs do not burn. (The cooked fish can be kept warm in a slow oven for about 15 minutes.)

3. Transfer to plates, garnish with lemon and parsley, and serve.

4 servings

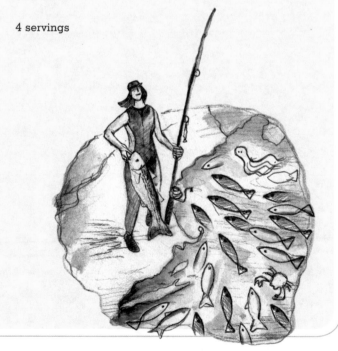

Roast Bluefish

Super-fresh bluefish is one of the highlights of a New England summer, and The Place is justly famous for theirs. The bluefish are caught in Long Island Sound by the chef-owner brothers themselves or by one of the staff, cleaned and rinsed in ice and seawater right on the boat, and rushed to the restaurant, where the fillets are cooked as they do everything else — by simply grill-roasting them with lemon and butter. When the catch is fresh that day, The Place hoists their "bluefish burgee" out front — a pennant made by a loyal bluefish-obsessed customer. They give you a hefty serving of everything at The Place (upward of 12 ounces of fish), but I have scaled back the portion size.

4   **bluefish fillets, 6 to 8 ounces each**

1   **lemon, thinly sliced**

4   **tablespoons butter**

Salt and freshly ground black pepper

1. Prepare a moderately hot hardwood or charcoal fire, or preheat a gas grill.

2. Place each piece of fish on a sheet of aluminum foil large enough to enclose it. Divide the lemon slices over the fish, top each with 1 tablespoon of butter, and season well with salt and pepper. Wrap the foil around the fish (not too tightly) and crimp the edges to close.

3. Place the foil packets on the grill, crimped-sides up, and cook until the fish is opaque, about 15 minutes. (When the packets emit a puff of steam when pierced with a small knife, the fish is probably done. Open and check if need be.)

4. Open the foil packet slightly when serving.

4 servings

Broiled Mackerel

When the mackerel are running near Provincetown, Jerry Carreiro cooks the fresh fish by simply broiling or oven roasting with a bit of lemon butter. The succulent, oily flesh of mackerel turns sweet and pearly white when cooked, and when Jerry has mackerel on his menu at Tip For Tops'n, word gets out quickly and a steady stream of fish lovers beats a path to his door.

4   **large or 8 small mackerel, cleaned and split or filleted (see Note)**

4   **tablespoons butter**

1   **tablespoon lemon juice**

Paprika

Lemon wedges

1. Preheat the broiler. Arrange the fish skin-side down on an oiled broiler pan.

2. Melt the butter and stir in the lemon juice. Brush the fish with the lemon butter and sprinkle with the paprika.

3. Broil, 4 to 5 inches from the element until the fish is cooked through and lightly browned on top, 5 to 8 minutes.

4. Serve with the lemon wedges.

NOTE: The small mackerel bones can be pesky but are not too difficult to eat around. A very expert fish filleter can remove the entire backbone before the mackerel is cooked by cutting down either side of the bone and lifting it out.

4 servings

Land Ho!

Orleans, Massachusetts

From Land Ho!

WELLFLEET OYSTERS ON THE HALF SHELL (PAGE 29)
CREAMY CAPE COD CLAM CHOWDER (PAGE 60)
KALE SOUP (PAGE 77)
BROILED BLUEFISH DIJONNAISE (PAGE 136)
CLAM PIE (PAGE 174)

I f you ask "real food" connoisseurs to reveal the names of their favorite year-round places on Cape Cod, Land Ho! always shows up at or near the top of everyone's list. This saloon-cum-restaurant is a mid-Cape institution, owned and operated by the Murphy family for 40 years. It's always crowded with locals and tourists, and there's often a wait. But the service is so efficient and friendly and the food so consistently good that it's well worth it. I can't do better than quote my food-lovin', Cape Cod–vacationin' friend Dale Burmeister's description: "Land Ho! is a noisy, colorful place, and we generally go there the day we arrive. It's the official starting gun for our vacation. The menu is a mile long and changes daily and is written in colored chalks on a big blackboard hanging above the bar. The galley kitchen

is open to view. Three cooks just fit in, and they pump out a tremendous volume and variety and never look hassled. The chowder is great. Wonderful clam pie, plus all the usual fried seafood, as well as a lot of broiled — all fresh and good. We're never happier than when they have fresh broiled bluefish on the menu. It's always been caught that day and is served with a very nice dijonnaise sauce on a pile of terrific mashed potatoes and a side of fresh asparagus. I wish I were there right now!"

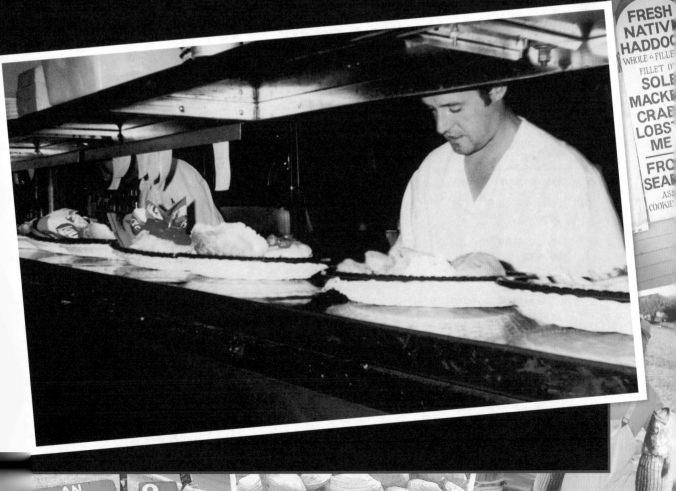

Wood-Grilled Barbecued Chicken

Everything at Guilford, Connecticut's, The Place is cooked over their 25-foot-long wood-fired grill. Mostly, it's fresh seafood, but for non–fish fanciers (or just for a change of pace), there's nothing more delicious than their smoky-sweet barbecued chicken breast. Gary Knowles gets 10-ounce breast halves and has them boned out but leaves on the skin to trap juiciness and flavor. Although he's tried several types of commercial barbecue sauce, Gary keeps coming back to Ken's brand, which is not available in retail markets, so I've provided a reasonable facsimile thereof. It's got a good sweet-tangy-hot balance and a smooth consistency that creates a nice bond with the meat.

Smooth-and-Tangy Tomato Barbecue Sauce

¼	cup tomato paste
2	cups water
⅔	cup corn syrup
⅓	cup cider vinegar
¼	cup vegetable oil
2	teaspoons Worcestershire sauce
1	teaspoon garlic powder
1	teaspoon onion powder
¾	teaspoon salt
¼ to ½	teaspoon cayenne pepper

Chicken

4	large chicken breast halves, boneless, but with skin on

1. For the sauce, in a medium saucepan, whisk together the tomato paste and water. Add the corn syrup, vinegar, oil, Worcestershire sauce, garlic powder, onion powder, and salt and whisk to combine. Bring to a boil, reduce the heat to medium-low, and simmer, uncovered, for about 15 minutes, until the sauce is lightly thickened and the flavors are blended. Stir in the cayenne (use the greater amount for a spicier sauce) and simmer for 2 to 3 minutes. The recipe will make about 2 cups of sauce. Store leftover sauce in the refrigerator for up to 2 weeks.

2. To cook the chicken, build a moderately hot hardwood or charcoal fire or preheat a gas grill.

Continued on next page

3. Place the chicken breasts on the grill, skin-side down, and cook for about 5 minutes. Turn skin-side up and cook for about 5 more minutes, or until the chicken is about half cooked.

4. Spoon about ½ cup of the sauce into a small dish. Brush the skin side generously with sauce, turn, and brush the undersides with sauce. Cook until the skin is crisped and slightly blackened in spots and the chicken is cooked through, 5 to 10 minutes, depending on the thickness of the chicken and the heat of the fire.

5. Serve with additional barbecue sauce on the side, if desired.

4 servings

THE OCEAN STATE

Rhode Island's nickname is the Ocean State. Measuring only 48 miles north to south and 37 miles east to west, it is the smallest state in the United States. However, a considerable portion of Rhode Island's real estate fronts the Atlantic Ocean and the wide, deeply convoluted Narragansett Bay. Because of all its inlets, peninsulas, and bays, it's estimated that the coastline of Rhode Island adds up to more than 400 miles.

CHAPTER 7

One-Dish Seafood Wonders

New England's historic superabundance of fresh seafood has mandated that cooks in the region find ways of using that splendid harvest of the sea in many and sundry creative guises — mostly, in the past, as a way to use up leftovers. The remains of the broiled fish from last night's dinner were combined with mashed potato and seasonings to become tonight's fish cakes; crab picked on Thursday was tossed with breadcrumbs and shaped into crab cakes for Friday; plentiful (and cheap) clams were minced and baked into a crust to become a midweek clam pie. Portuguese New Englanders simmered less tender cuts of pork in a spicy sauce and then finished the dish with a few briny hardshell clams, and Italian Americans stewed sweet calamari (which had been rejected by mainstream New Englanders) in garlicky tomato sauces. Then there is the practice of making casseroles out of cooked seafood bound with a rich cream sauce and a topping of luxurious buttered crumbs — a tradition that lives on in the present tense. These days, restaurants and home cooks don't rely on leftovers to make these much-loved (and often do-ahead) dishes, but delight in showcasing them as some of the most interesting and tasty food of the region.

Calamari Fra Diavolo

This is what my husband, a calamari connoisseur, ordered the first time we went to the Seahorse Tavern in Noank, Connecticut, and after one bite of the perfectly balanced sauce and tender tentacles, I put this dish on my list of "must-have" recipes from the Seahorse kitchen. Chef-owner Bob Sader kindly shared it, along with a tip: If you buy the calamari frozen, partially thaw the package in cold water and then cut the bodies into rings. They're easier to slice when still slightly frozen.

2   tablespoons butter

2   tablespoons olive oil

2 to 3 garlic cloves, finely chopped

½   teaspoon crushed red pepper flakes, or to taste

2   pounds calamari, tentacles detached, bodies sliced into rings

3   cups Seahorse Marinara sauce (following page)

Salt and freshly ground black pepper

1   pound angel hair pasta

½   cup thinly sliced scallions

1. Heat the butter and oil in a very large skillet. Add the garlic and pepper flakes and cook over medium-high heat, stirring, for 30 seconds. Add the calamari tentacles and rings and cook, stirring, until coated with oil and beginning to turn opaque, about 3 minutes. Add the marinara sauce, bring to a boil, reduce the heat, and simmer for about 10 minutes, until the calamari is cooked through and the flavors blend. Season with salt and pepper to taste.

2. Meanwhile, bring a large pot of salted water to a boil for the pasta. Cook the pasta at a rapid boil until al dente, about 6 minutes. Drain in a colander.

3. In a large bowl or rimmed platter, toss the pasta with the sauce. Sprinkle with scallions and serve.

4 to 6 servings

Seahorse Marinara

The secret here, you'll notice, is to *not* simmer this sauce for a long time, thus preserving the fresh taste and texture of the meaty, flavorful plum tomatoes. Be sure to use a good imported brand for best results.

6   tablespoons olive oil

1   tablespoon finely chopped garlic

1   can (8 ounces) tomato purée

2   tablespoons chopped fresh basil, or 1 teaspoon dried

3   large (28- to 32-ounce) cans plum tomatoes and juice

Salt and freshly ground black pepper

Pinches of sugar

1. In a large pot, heat the oil. Add the garlic and cook over medium heat about 1 minute. Add the tomato purée and basil. Cook, stirring frequently, for 10 minutes.

2. Lift the plum tomatoes out of their liquid and squeeze with your fingers to break them into smaller pieces, or chop them with a knife. Add the tomatoes and most of their juice. Bring the sauce to the boil.

3. Remove from heat and season to taste with salt and pepper. If the sauce tastes at all bitter, add a little sugar. (The sauce can be made ahead and held at cool room temperature for several hours, refrigerated for 2 to 3 days, or frozen.)

Makes about 2 quarts

HAPPY IN THEIR WORK

When you enter Anne Miller's domain at the Cod End Cookhouse in Tenants Harbor, Maine, you sense immediately that it's a well-managed operation. "I've got a great kitchen," she says. One female employee who is the onion ring specialist, says, "This is a good summer job. We all get along in here and Anne is a good boss. Yes, I do begin to get a little tired of onion rings 'long about the middle of August [as she carefully and deftly breads and fries her 55th batch that day], but I don't mind. It's a short season here, but good money, too, while it lasts."

Tip For Tops'n

Provincetown, Massachusetts

From Tip For Tops'n
BROILED MACKEREL (PAGE 153)
CARREIRO'S PORK WITH CLAMS (PAGE 164)
PORTUGUESE BREAD PUDDING (PAGE 227)

Everything about Carreiro's Tip For Tops'n restaurant is completely straightforward — except the name, which, owner Jerry Carreiro explains, was inherited from the previous owners, and refers to top food and service at the tip of the Cape. It is that, for sure, and much more. Tip For Tops'n, which has been run by the Carreiros since 1965, is one of the last family-run Portuguese restaurants on Cape Cod.

The nautical-themed dining room with booths and varnished wood walls is attractive and inviting and service is friendly, low-key, and efficient. The extensive lunch and dinner menus list all manner of broiled and fried seafood, steaks, and American fare, like burgers and club sandwiches, as well as such Portuguese special-

ties as kale soup, Portuguese mussels, pork with clams, fried sole in "our own Portuguese sauce," and *caldeirada,* a bouillabaisse-like Portuguese seafood stew — all made from recipes passed down from Carreiro's grandmother. The Portuguese-style baked stuffed sole with a sea clam stuffing is incredibly delicious. (The menu describes the stuffing as "an authentic and original fisherman's recipe, blending the flavors of shrimp, scallops, lobster, and wine with a light seasoning of special herbs.") A lovely earthenware dish holds the scrumptious spicy pork with little-necks and potatoes, which I managed to polish off despite the enormous portion. Homemade desserts include fruit pies, molten chocolate pudding, and a warm, egg-rich Portuguese bread pudding. And to top it off, you can return the next morning for an all-American diner-type breakfast or spicy Portuguese linguiça sausage and eggs.

Carreiro's Pork with Clams

It's called *carne de porco a alentajana* in Portuguese, and it's one of the most interesting and tasty dishes ever to make its way across the Atlantic and settle in New England. This is an adaptation of the Pork with Clams served at the Carreiros' family restaurant, Tip For Tops'n, in Provincetown — and it's a decidedly and deliciously spicy version. At the restaurant, they use Frank's Hot Sauce, which is thick with puréed peppers and only moderately hot. Tabasco or other liquid hot pepper sauce can be substituted, but you'll have to vary the amounts according to your heat tolerance.

Marinade and Pork

1¼ cups dry white wine

½ cup liquid hot pepper sauce

3 tablespoons minced garlic

1 teaspoon paprika

1 teaspoon salt

3 pounds boneless pork, such as butt or shoulder, cut in 1½-inch cubes

To Cook and Finish

⅔ cup extra-virgin olive oil

2 tablespoons minced garlic

1 cup water

7 cups diced unpeeled russet potatoes

24 littleneck clams, scrubbed

Lemon wedges

1. For the marinade, in a large bowl, stir together the wine, hot pepper sauce, garlic, paprika, and salt. Add the pork, toss to coat, and refrigerate for at least 24 hours.

2. In a large pot, heat ⅓ cup of the olive oil. Add the garlic, and cook, stirring, for 1 minute. Add the pork, with its marinade, and the water. Bring to a boil, stirring, reduce the heat to low, and cook, covered, until the pork is tender, 1¼ to 1½ hours.

3. Preheat the oven to 425°F. On a large, rimmed baking sheet, toss the cubed potatoes with the remaining ⅓ cup of olive oil. Roast in the preheated oven until the potatoes are tender and beginning to brown, about 20 minutes.

4. Scrape the potatoes into a large earthenware casserole or glass baking dish. Pour the pork and juices over the potatoes and arrange the clams in a single layer on the top. Bake, uncovered, in the preheated oven just until the clams pop open, about 10 minutes. Garnish with lemon wedges and serve directly from the baking dish.

6 servings

Crab Cakes

They deep-fry their crab cakes at J.T. Farnham's in Essex, Massachusetts, but owner Terry Cellucci says that if she's doing it at home, she panfries them. Either way, these cakes are a really good balance of fresh crab bound with just the right amount of crumbs and (at J.T's) locally produced fresh eggs. If you ask your server, your order will come with a little pleated paper cup of some knock-your-socks-off red hot sauce on the side.

2 **pounds fresh crab-meat, picked over**

2 **eggs, lightly beaten**

1 **cup breadcrumbs**

1 **cup crushed Hi-Ho or Ritz cracker crumbs (about ¾ of a sleeve)**

½ **cup chopped red pepper**

1 **tablespoon Old Bay or other mixed sea-food seasoning**

1 **teaspoon salt**

1 **teaspoon freshly ground black pepper**

1 **teaspoon paprika**

1 **tablespoon chopped parsley**

1 **tablespoon lemon juice**

1 **teaspoon Worcestershire sauce**

2 to 3 tablespoons butter

2 to 3 tablespoons light olive oil

Lemon wedges

Liquid hot pepper sauce

1. In a large bowl, combine the crabmeat, eggs, breadcrumbs, cracker crumbs, red pepper, Old Bay, salt, pepper, paprika, parsley, lemon juice, and Worcestershire sauce. Use a wooden spoon or clean hands to mix lightly but thoroughly. Scoop out ⅓ cup of mixture for each cake and shape into ½-inch-thick patties. (Patties can be refrigerated for several hours.)

2. In two large skillets, heat 2 tablespoons each of the butter and oil over medium heat. Cook the crab cakes until nicely browned and crusty on the bottom, 3 to 4 minutes. Turn and continue to cook until the underside is browned and the crab cakes are thoroughly hot in the center, about 5 more minutes. Use the remaining butter and oil to cook any remaining cakes.

3. Serve hot, with lemon wedges and hot pepper sauce.

6 servings (3 crab cakes per serving)

Cod End Fish Cakes

Fish cakes have been a Yankee staple for at least a couple of centuries, and Anne Miller, owner and prime mover behind the Cod End Cookhouse in Tenants Harbor, Maine, added them to her menu "because I love fish cakes" — and her lucky customers are the beneficiaries. She uses local hake because she can always get it fresh and because it flakes so easily, but at home you can make these simple and delicious, dill-flecked cakes with just about any fish, freshly cooked or left over.

1½ pounds russet or all-purpose potatoes, peeled and cut in 2-inch chunks

1 pound hake fillets, or a similar lean white-fish that flakes easily

½ cup finely chopped onion

1 garlic clove, finely chopped

3 tablespoons snipped fresh dill

2 teaspoons Old Bay or other seafood seasoning blend

½ teaspoon liquid hot pepper sauce (see Note)

Salt and freshly ground black pepper

3 to 4 tablespoons safflower or other vegetable oil

Tartar sauce

Lemon wedges

1. Bring a large pot of salted water to the boil. Cook the potatoes at a boil until very soft, about 20 minutes. Drain well and put the potatoes through a ricer or coarsely mash them with a potato masher. You should have about 4 cups of mashed potatoes.

2. Meanwhile, cook the fish in barely simmering salted water to cover until it flakes easily, 5 to 10 minutes, depending on thickness. Drain. When cool enough to handle, break or chop the fish into flakes no larger than about ¾ inch.

3. In a large bowl, combine the potato and hake. Add the onion, garlic, dill, Old Bay seasoning, and hot pepper sauce. Mix gently but thoroughly to combine. Season to taste with salt and pepper.

4. Shape the mixture into eight cakes about ½ inch thick. (The cakes can be made up to 4 hours ahead. Cover and refrigerate.)

5. Heat the oil in a large skillet over medium heat. When the oil is hot, add the fish cakes to the pan and cook, in two batches if necessary, until browned on both sides and heated through, 7 to 10 minutes total.

6. Serve with tartar sauce and lemon wedges.

NOTE: At Cod End, they use Tabasco hot sauce.

4 servings

SWEET NEW ENGLAND CRAB

Most crabs caught in New England are sand or rock crabs. In Maine, sand crabs are often referred to generically as "Maine crabs," but sometimes they were called "picked-toe" (local slang for pointed-toe) crabs. At high-end New York restaurants, the name evolved into "peekytoe." In Rhode Island and Massachusetts, these same crabs are known as "Jonah crabs."

Because New England crabs are relatively small, "picking out" steamed crabs is a time-consuming and painstaking task that requires skill and practice to do well. In Maine, women working in small licensed home operations do most of the picking, and signs for fresh crabmeat can be spotted along the highways in the summer. "Lots of women like doing this," says Sandy White of Brooklin, Maine. "We can work at home, care for our children as we work, be our own boss." If you can't get fresh-picked crabmeat, use good pasteurized lump-style crabmeat.

Quito's Restaurant

Bristol, Rhode Island

From Quito's

LITTLENECKS WITH OIL AND GARLIC (PAGE 36)

BAKED SCROD WITH LEMON-GARLIC CRUMBS (PAGE 141)

FRANK FORMISANO'S SEAFOOD MEDITERRANEAN (PAGE 171)

A few years ago Frank Formisano joined forces with Al Quito, whose parents had started a simple fish market — and later small restaurant — on Bristol harbor in the 1950s. They expanded the seating and Frank added some of his grandparents' cherished Mediterranean-style seafood dishes to their repertoire — grafting them onto what had been pretty much an all-fried seafood menu — and the combined result is now what might be described as Rhode Island culinary nirvana.

The place is still right on Bristol harbor, and it's still simple, but very attractive. The smallish indoor dining room is exceptionally pleasant, with varnished bead board wainscoting and a blackboard of daily specials. On a warm summer night, however, I can't imagine a more heavenly spot than Quito's patio, seated beneath the twinkling clam shell lights, drinking in the view of passing sailboats and kayakers and listening to the lap of waves. Efficient, friendly waitresses ply both

rooms and are always ready to describe and recommend their menu favorites.

Quito's (derived from the Italian name Guido, so pronounced *gwee-does*) serves up an excellent house-made creamy clam chowder — one of the best I've ever tasted — and all of their more typically New England–style fare is outstanding, including steamed clams, whole-belly and clam strip rolls, fried scallops, steamed lobsters and lobster rolls, and a lovely lemon and garlic crumbed baked scrod. And of course such Rhode Island specialties as clam cakes, fried calamari with hot pepper rings, and stuffed quahogs are de rigueur on any Ocean State menu. But it's Frank Formisano's Seafood Mediterranean that is the most popular menu item. You can order the seafood — calamari, shrimp, scallops, and mussels — either sautéed or fried (pure caloric indulgence, but fabulous) — and it is then bathed in a zesty and beautifully balanced marinara sauce, replete with kalamata olives and hot pepper rings. This dish is a wonder.

Old-Fashioned Salt Codfish Cakes

When I got this recipe from the Maine Diner I thought there might be some mistake. The received wisdom about dried salt cod is that it needs to be softened and de-salted by soaking in water for several hours before cooking. But the kitchen said no, they don't soak, just simmer the cod for about 20 minutes and then shred it fine in a food processor. Brilliant! It's much more flavorful than the water-soaked fish, and the processor takes care of any potential toughness. Once you make codfish cakes this way, I bet you'll never go back.

½ **pound salt cod**

4 **tablespoons (½ stick) butter**

1 **cup chopped onions**

3 **cups mashed potatoes (see Note)**

½ **cup instant potato flakes or buds**

1 **egg**

¼ **teaspoon white pepper**

4 **tablespoons light olive oil or vegetable oil**

1. Cut the cod into 2- or 3-inch chunks. Place in a saucepan, cover with water, and bring to a boil. Reduce the heat and simmer, covered, until fairly tender, about 20 minutes. Drain, remove any skin and bones, and pulse in a food processor until finely shredded.

2. In a medium skillet, melt the butter. Add the onions and sauté over medium heat until softened, about 5 minutes.

3. In a large bowl, combine the cod, onions, mashed potatoes, potato flakes, egg, and pepper. (The potato flakes help hold the cakes together.) Use your hands or a wooden spoon to mix thoroughly. Using about ½ cup for each cake, shape into 10 to 12 cakes about ¾-inch high. Place on a baking pan and refrigerate for at least 2 hours or overnight.

4. Heat the oil in one large or two medium skillets. Cook the cakes over medium heat until nicely browned, turning carefully with a spatula, about 10 minutes total, and serve.

NOTE: Boil 2 pounds all-purpose potatoes and mash with 2 tablespoons butter and ½ cup milk.

4 to 6 servings

Frank Formisano's Seafood Mediterranean

In order to begin to re-create the Quito's dish you must start with a really good homemade marinara sauce and move on from there. Chef Frank Formisano then stirs in garlic butter, meaty kalamata olives, and sliced pickled peppers (for that typically Rhode Island touch) before adding the fresh seafood. You can use any combination of seafood that you like — all calamari happens to be great.

2	tablespoons butter
2	garlic cloves, minced
4	cups marinara sauce, such as Seahorse Marinara, page 161
20	pitted kalamata olives, halved
30	pickled Italian pepper rings (see Note)
1½	pounds mussels, scrubbed
½	pound calamari rings and tentacles
½	pound peeled medium shrimp
½	pound scallops (bay or sea)
1	pound spaghetti

1. In a large pot, melt the butter. Add the garlic and cook over medium heat, stirring, for 30 seconds. Add the tomato sauce, olives, and pepper rings and simmer for 10 minutes to blend flavors.

2. Add the seafood, bring to a boil, reduce the heat to low, and cook, covered, until the mussel shells open, 5 to 10 minutes.

3. Meanwhile, cook the spaghetti in a large pot of boiling salted water until al dente, about 10 minutes.

4. Ladle the sauce over the pasta, toss gently, and serve.

NOTE: Most establishments in Rhode Island, including Quito's, use *anelli di pepperoni*, which are mildly hot pickled Italian yellow banana peppers sliced into rings. As a substitute you might try thinly sliced pickled Italian cherry peppers or about half the amount of pickled jalapeño peppers.

4 to 5 servings

Crumb-Topped Lobster Pie

New Englanders make a few different versions of lobster pie. Sometimes it's lobster meat in an actual pie crust, sometimes it's more like a pot pie, with the lobster suspended in cream sauce (See Shaw's Lobster Pot Pie, page 179), but this one from the Maine Diner is a traditional old-fashioned lobster pie recipe that's been in the Henry family for many years. It's simple and straightforward — lobster meat, butter, Ritz cracker crumbs — but with the crucial addition of lobster tomalley, which is so full of rich lobster flavor that you won't believe the difference it makes in the final dish.

Four 1½-pound lobsters

1   **tablespoon salt**

12   **tablespoons (1½ sticks) butter, plus 6 tablespoons for serving**

2½   **cups crushed Ritz crackers**

Juice of 1 lemon

Freshly ground black pepper

Parsley sprigs

Lemon wedges

1. Bring 2 inches of water to a boil in a large pot. Add 1 tablespoon salt and plunge the lobsters into the water, heads down. Cover, return to the boil, reduce heat to medium, and steam for 12 minutes. Drain, reserving about ¾ cup of the cooking water. When cool enough to handle, pick the meat out of the lobsters, working over a bowl to catch any juices. Remove and reserve the green tomalley. Cut meat into 1½-inch chunks.

2. Melt the 12 tablespoons butter in a large skillet. Add the cracker crumbs and cook over medium-high heat, stirring often, until heated through. Stir in the tomalley. Squeeze in the lemon juice and add enough reserved lobster juices and cooking liquid to make a mixture that is about as moist as turkey stuffing. Season with salt and pepper to taste.

Maine Diner had its first customer come by accident. Literally. At least he stayed to have a meal with his coffee.

SLOW

(A RE-ENACTMENT)

3. Divide the lobster meat among four individual buttered ramekins or place in a shallow buttered 1½-quart baking dish. Cover with the cracker mixture, patting it on evenly. (Can be prepared up to 8 hours ahead and refrigerated. Remove from the refrigerator an hour or so before baking.)

4. Preheat the oven to 425°F. Bake the casserole(s) until the top begins to brown and the lobster is heated through, 10 to 15 minutes. Garnish with parsley and lemon wedges and serve the remaining 6 tablespoons butter, melted, alongside. You can squeeze lemon and drizzle butter over the lobster meat after it's out from under its crumb blanket.

4 servings

Fisherman's Fare

"DURING FISHING SEASON I get up at four A.M., slam three sandwiches together, and off I go. We usually leave the dock by 4:30. I have one sandwich for breakfast, one about ten A.M., and one for lunch."

— **Paul Sewall**
Captain, lobster boat *Franny Ellen*,
Stonington, Maine

Clam Pie

Clam pie is a good old Cape Cod dish, one that in days of yore, when clams were practically free, would have been served up as a simple workaday family supper. This delicious clam pie is adapted from an heirloom "receipt" that has been in the family files of Olive Jean Ellis Murphy (wife of Land Ho! owner John Murphy) for generations.

Pastry for double-crust pie, such as New England Lard Crust (page 206)

2½ pounds drained chopped sea clams

6 to 8 cups crushed Ritz crackers (4 to 5 sleeves of crackers)

½ cup finely chopped onion

¼ cup finely chopped celery

1 tablespoon finely chopped garlic

1 egg

1 tablespoon liquid hot pepper sauce (see Note)

1 tablespoon lemon juice

¼ teaspoon Old Bay or other seafood seasoning blend

¼ teaspoon white pepper

¾ cup (1½ sticks) butter, melted

Lemon wedges

1. Roll out one disk of the pastry and ease into a deep 9-inch pie plate. Refrigerate.

2. In a large bowl, combine the clams, 6 cups of cracker crumbs, onion, celery, and garlic. Toss to combine. In a small bowl, lightly beat the egg. Whisk in the hot pepper sauce, lemon juice, Old Bay, and white pepper. Add to the clam mixture and toss to combine. Drizzle with melted butter and toss and stir with a large fork to combine well. If the filling is very wet (depending on the juiciness of the clams), add 1 to 2 more cups of crumbs.

3. Preheat the oven to 350°F. Roll out the remaining disk of pastry dough. Spoon the clam filling into the pie shell, top with the top crust, fold the edges under, and crimp to seal. Cut several slashes in the top crust so that steam can escape.

4. Bake in the preheated oven until the crust is golden brown and the filling is heated through, 45 to 55 minutes. Cool on a wire rack for 10 to 30 minutes, cut into wedges, and serve, accompanied by lemon wedges.

NOTE: At Land Ho!, they use Frank's Hot Sauce, but Tabasco or another brand can be substituted.

8 servings

J.T. Farnham's

Essex, Massachusetts

From J.T. Fa...

NANA'S HADDOCK CHOW...
CRAB CAKES (PAGE 165)
AUNT NANCY'S COLESLAW

J.T. Farnham's is the real thing. This establishment has played an important role in North Shore clam shack history for the early years. In fact, according to local lore, it migh... actually have been one of the Farnham boys who came up with the idea to fry the first clam back in 1916 — but since the event occurred at Lawrence "Chubby" Woodman's place up the road, the historical edge goes to Woodman's. Whatever — the fact that this unassuming roadside restaurant has been frying up some of the most wonderful clams on the North Shore clam belt for all these years is good enough for us. The old-fashioned wood-frame structure is right on the road but faces back on a lovely tidal marsh. Terry and Joseph Cellucci bought J.T.'s in 1994 from the Farnham family, and they wisely decided to maintain the charming simplicity of the place — and although

much of the menu remains replete with such classic clam shack standards as classic New England haddock chowder, whole-belly fried clams, fish and chips, onion rings, and a delicious coleslaw, they've also added some newer items, such as a really good, chock-full-of-crab cake and a delectable (and very spicy) red scallop chowder. You place your order at the counter, and can take your food out to one of the picnic tables facing the marsh or sit inside in the clean and pleasingly plain indoor dining room. Either way, you'll stand in line with vacationers and locals, which is part of the pleasant, low-key, in-the-rough experience that is J.T. Farnham's.

Lobster Pot Pie

At Shaw's, their lobster pot pie is something like a lobster gratin — a rich and luxurious dish in itself — made more so with its buttery crumb topping. Because it can be made ahead and reheated just before serving, this lobster pot pie makes an ideal meal for a special dinner party.

Lobster and Cream Sauce

4   cups cooked lobster meat, cut in chunks (from four 1¼-pound lobsters)

3   tablespoons butter

3   tablespoons all-purpose flour

3   cups heavy cream

½   cup medium-dry sherry

½   teaspoon paprika

Salt and freshly ground black pepper

Crumb Topping

1½ cups crushed Ritz cracker crumbs (about 1 sleeve of crackers)

3   tablespoons butter, melted

½   teaspoon paprika

1. Divide the lobster meat into four shallow 8-ounce ramekins or gratin dishes, or place in a 1½-quart shallow baking dish.

2. In a large saucepan, melt the butter over medium-high heat. Add the flour and cook, whisking, until bubbly, about 1 minute. Add the cream and sherry, bring just to the boil, and cook, whisking, until the mixture is thick and bubbly. Season with the paprika and with salt and pepper to taste. Pour the sauce over the lobster in the dishes. The sauce will thicken as it cools.

3. For the topping, toss the cracker crumbs with the melted butter and paprika until well mixed. (The pies and topping can be made up to several hours ahead to this point and refrigerated.)

4. Preheat the oven to 425°F. Sprinkle the crumbs evenly over the lobster mixture. Bake, uncovered, in the preheated oven until the sauce is bubbly and the crumbs are deep golden brown, 10 to 15 minutes for ramekins, 15 to 20 minutes for a large baking dish.

4 servings

with

CHAPTER 8

Traditional Accompaniments

What's apple pie without the cheese, what's a kiss without the squeeze, and what's a New England fried seafood dinner without . . . tartar sauce, coleslaw, onion rings, and fries? They are de rigueur — as are the other condiments that are usually set out on the clam shack counter, such as lemon wedges, cider or malt vinegar (great for sprinkling on all fried food), and, in Rhode Island, pickled hot Italian peppers. One of the distinguishing marks of your better-than-average clam shack, lobster pound, or chowder house is that someone in charge has insisted that it is well worth going to that extra trouble of making their own from-scratch versions instead of opening up a vat of gloppy commercial salad or buying ready-battered onion rings. These are simple, straightforward, uncomplicated side dishes, but it takes time and effort to ensure that they're made well. And that's precisely what separates the first-rate eatery from the ordinary, unexceptional establishment.

Aunt Nancy's Coleslaw

Coleslaw competition is fierce among all the various clam shack–type establishments on Massachusetts' North Shore, which means that all their lucky customers get to reap the delicious, homemade rewards. This is the version you get at J.T. Farnham's in Essex, and it's a tried-and-true Cellucci family recipe. It's got just the right amount of sweetness from the pineapple, counterbalanced by the pleasantly bitter bite of a little bit of celery seed.

¾ **cup mayonnaise (see Note)**

¼ **cup sugar**

1½ **teaspoons white vinegar**

¾ **teaspoon celery seed**

1 **small carrot, coarsely chopped**

1 **can (4 ounces) chunk pineapple, partially drained**

1 **medium head (1½ pounds) shredded cabbage (about 8 cups)**

Salt and freshly ground black pepper

1. In a large bowl, whisk together the mayonnaise, sugar, vinegar, and celery seed.

2. In the work bowl of a food processor, combine the carrot and pineapple. Pulse lightly to make a coarsely textured mixture. Add the pineapple mixture to the bowl, along with the cabbage, and toss. Season with salt and pepper to taste.

3. Refrigerate for at least 1 hour. Spoon off excess liquid before serving.

NOTE: At J.T. Farnham's, they use Cain's brand mayonnaise.

4 to 6 servings

Double-Dipped Onion Rings

Onion rings are a requisite part of the clam shack experience, and the crispy, slightly puffy, deeply golden rings at Bagaduce Lunch, a little clam shack in Penobscot, Maine, are some of the best ever. The secret to good onion rings is simple, says owner Mike Astbury. Use freshly cut "colossal" onions and thoroughly bread them twice before they hit the fryer.

Vegetable oil for frying

1   large onion, cut
     crosswise about
     ¼ inch thick

Cold water

1½ cups breading mix
     (see Note)

1. Heat the oil in a deep fryer or deep pot to 375°F. Fill the fryer or pot no more than half full of oil.

2. Separate the onion into rings. Put the water into one large bowl and the breading mix into another bowl. Dip about half the onions into the cold water. Lift out, shaking off the excess, and dredge in the breading mix, shaking off the excess. Repeat the process, dipping again into the water and then in the breading. If the breading mix is clumpy, shake off excess in a colander.

3. Slide the rings into the fryer. Stand back; because of their high moisture content, onion rings can spatter. Cook, turning with tongs, until the onions are a deep golden brown, 2 to 3 minutes. Drain on paper towels. Repeat with the rest of the onions.

4. Serve while hot.

NOTE: Bagaduce uses a breading mix containing flour, corn flour, nonfat dry milk, sodium bicarbonate, salt, and powdered egg whites. Look for one with similar ingredients.

2 servings

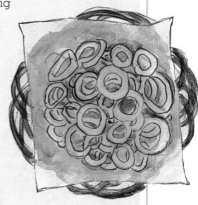

Casseroled "Baked Stuffed" Clam Stuffing

Maureen Woodman, one of many Woodman family members who help run the business even all these many years after its founding, provided their hugely popular recipe for clam stuffing. No, sadly, baked stuffed clams don't appear on Woodman's regular menu, but this stuffing is a menu option at the function room behind the restaurant and is also now available from their retail shop freezer. Instead of filling clam shells, which can crack in the oven, Woodman's does this bacon-redolent, clam-laden stuffing casserole-style.

¼	pound (6 or 7 slices) bacon
4	tablespoons butter
½	cup chopped red or white onions
1	tablespoon chopped garlic
3	cups chopped drained hard-shell clams with juice
3	cups crushed Ritz cracker crumbs (two sleeves of crackers)
3	tablespoons grated Parmesan cheese

Juice of 1 lemon

1. Grease an 8-inch square baking dish. Preheat the oven to 350°F.

2. In a large skillet, cook the bacon over medium-low heat until crisp and the fat is rendered, about 10 minutes. Remove with a slotted spoon to drain on paper towels, leaving about 3 tablespoons drippings in the pan. Crumble the bacon and reserve.

3. Add the butter to the skillet. Add the onions and garlic and sauté over medium heat until the onions begin to soften, about 2 minutes. Add the clams with their juice and cook, stirring, until the clams turn white and the liquid is somewhat reduced, about 5 minutes. Stir in the crumbs, Parmesan, lemon juice, and reserved bacon and mix thoroughly. The stuffing should be stiff but not dry. If too loose, add a quarter cup or so more crumbs; if too dry, add a bit of water. Spoon into the prepared baking dish. (Can be made up to a day ahead. Cover and refrigerate.)

4. Bake the casserole, uncovered, in the preheated oven until the stuffing is golden brown and crusty, 35 to 40 minutes. Cut into squares or spoon out to serve.

6 to 8 side-dish servings

Aggelakis Tartar Sauce

What's a fried clam without tartar sauce to dip it in? Like love and marriage, many people believe you can't have one without the other. And if you needed one more good reason to patronize the Clam Box in Ipswich, just add to the list the fact that owner Chickie Aggelakis makes her own.

1¼ cups mayonnaise (see Note)

¼ cup drained sweet pickle relish

2 tablespoons ground or finely chopped sweet onion, such as Spanish or Vidalia

1. In a small bowl, stir together the mayonnaise, relish, and onion.

2. Refrigerate for at least 2 hours before serving or for up to 1 week.

NOTE: The Clam Box uses a rich, heavy commercial mayonnaise, but Hellmann's or Best Foods is a good substitute.

Makes 1½ cups

KEEP THE CHOWDER AND SLAW

From an editorial in the *Bangor* (Maine) *Daily News*: "It can come as a rude shock when you walk into a favorite restaurant around here and find total change. Instead of paper place mats with advertisements or lobster-picking instructions on them, there's a spotless tablecloth and fancy cloth napkins maybe stuck into a fancy napkin ring. There's a 'server' reciting specials and talk of 'reduction' sauces. For dessert, none of your bread pudding or lemon chiffon pie, but a chocolate mousse or crème brûlée. Don't count on finding an honest bowl of chowder. And when they say they don't serve coleslaw, that's the last straw.

"Still, there are some places left where you can get good plain food. . . .

"Of course, there are people who like the fancy menu and the fancy food. Let them have them. As long as the rest of us get to keep the chowder and slaw."

The Bite

Menemsha, Massachusetts

From The Bite

FRIED FLOUNDER (PAGE 145)
GRANDMA'S PICKLED BEETS (PAGE 196)
RED BLISS POTATO SALAD (PAGE 197)

The Bite is a darling little box of a place sitting right at the entrance road to Menemsha Beach on Martha's Vineyard. It's strictly takeout, so you step up onto the porch and order at the window from one of the cheery staff. Then you can sit at one of their picnic tables or do what most people do, which is wend your way with your tray the few hundred yards to the beach and have yourself one of the best beach meals you're likely to encounter anywhere. The menu is short and to the point: clam chowder (not too thick, made from a base supplied by the nearby Home Port restaurant) and fried seafood — whole-belly clams, plump sweet scallops, oysters, shrimp, squid, and the freshest, crustiest fried flounder you can imagine. That's about it.

(In Chilmark, on this part of the Vineyard, the various eating establishments have agreed to divide up their specialties — therefore, Larson's down the road, for instance, doesn't do fried seafood, and The Bite doesn't do lobster rolls.) But we mustn't forget The Bite's homemade side salads, for which they are also famous. Owner Karen Flynn's mother, Barbara, makes gallons of her wonderful dill-flecked potato salad every week, and the crispy-creamy coleslaw is a must-have with the fish and chips. And when Karen bought the place 16 years ago, her Lithuanian grand-mother insisted that she add pickled beets to the menu, where they have stayed to great local acclaim. (You should always listen to Grandma, Karen admits.) And if you fancy a little something sweet for dessert, pick up a few of the homemade "bite-sized" (get it?) fudge brownies or cookies.

RHODE ISLAND'S QUIRKY CUISINE

Rhode Islanders are passionate about their food. While much of their cuisine is similar to food found all over the rest of New England, Rhode Islanders have also developed many dishes (and the lingo to describe them) that are unique to the Ocean State. Since the eastern side of Narragansett Bay is also contiguous to South Coast Massachusetts, many of these specialties can be found just across the state line, too.

If you're not from this area, you may never have heard of:

Stuffies. Baked stuffed quahogs. Chopped hard-shell clams are combined with breadcrumbs, onions, peppers, seasonings, sometimes bacon or spicy linguiça sausage (the Portuguese contribution), piled back into the clamshell, and baked.

Clam cakes. Also called clam fritters. These bear no resemblance whatsoever to a delicate crab cake. Rather, they consist of chopped hard-shell clams embedded in a baking powder batter and deep-fried, so they emerge looking like rough-hewn brown golf balls. In Rhode Island, clam chowder is automatically served with an order of clam cakes. An old name for clam cakes was "boat steerers." A heavy, leaden clam fritter is derisively termed a "sinker."

Rhode Island red chowder. Many Rhode Island establishments will offer milky chowder, clear chowder, and their unique chowder variation, which adds tomato to the broth, tinting it red.

Doughboys. Small squares of puffy fried dough, served hot, and usually rolled in granulated sugar. May be derived from the similar Portuguese fried bread called *malassada.*

Chow Mein sandwiches. For the non–Rhode Islander, a truly weird concoction made by piling Chinese chow mein in a thick brown gravy on a hamburger bun and topping it with crisp chow mein noodles. Because the bun instantly starts to dissolve, knife and fork are usually a necessity.

Rhode Island lunch. A luncheonette specialty, this is a grilled hamburger bun filled with melted cheese and sprinkled with chopped onion and pickle.

Coffee milk. Sweet, concentrated coffee syrup (invented by a Rhode Island company in the early 1900s), stirred into cold milk. Coffee milk outsells chocolate milk four to one at Ocean State convenience stores.

Jonnycakes. That's right, there's no "h" in the spelling, which is protected by state law. These are pancakes made with White Cap Flint corn, which is stone-ground at Rhode Island gristmills. Jonnycakes are the staple of traditional May Breakfasts, which are staged as fund-raisers by volunteer organizations every year on the first weekend of May.

Del's Lemonade. Established in 1948, this company sells their slushy, slurpy sweet-tart drink from trucks, street carts, and shops all over the state. There's at least one real lemon peel in each cup.

Snail salad. Marinated slivers of cooked snail (or conch) tossed with diced vegetables and an oil and vinegar dressing. (Probably introduced into the local repertoire by the large contingent of Italian immigrants.)

Shakers of vinegar on the table. A dousing of vinegar (usually malt vinegar) on fried food is what differentiates a local from a visitor.

My Best Guess at Chickie's Coleslaw

I begged and pleaded with Clam Box owner Chickie Aggelakis. Sorry, she said, I'll give you any recipe — *except* my coleslaw. So I asked her if it would be okay if my friend and fellow coleslaw taster Barbara Keyes and I tried to come up with as similar a version as we could, and she said sure, fine, go ahead, make a stab at it. Well . . . we think it's pretty darn close, and awfully darn good. It's dedicated to you, Chickie.

¾ **cup mayonnaise (see Note)**

3 **tablespoons sugar**

2 **teaspoons celery salt**

1 **small head (about 1 pound) shredded cabbage (about 6 cups)**

¼ **cup shredded carrots**

1. In a large bowl, whisk together the mayonnaise, sugar, and celery salt. Add the cabbage and carrots; toss well to combine. Refrigerate for at least 2 hours or overnight.

2. Before serving, stir well and spoon off any excess liquid. Serve with a slotted spoon, leaving any additional liquid behind in the bowl.

NOTE: The Clam Box uses a rich, heavy commercial mayonnaise, but Hellmann's or Best Foods is a good substitute.

About 6 servings

Our Motto

"IF WE CAN'T SERVE THE BEST, then we won't serve anything!"

— Marina "Chickie" Aggelakis
Clam Box

Roast Corn

Gary Knowles, one of the chef-owner brothers at The Place in Guilford, Connecticut, says proudly, "Our corn is legendary. We serve thousands and thousands of ears every year." And what could be simpler? No husking, no removing the silk — just throw the whole ears on the grill and let them roast until the husks are blackened and crumbly and the kernels are imbued with the sweet smokiness of the fire. Could be one of the reasons The Place consistently wins *Connecticut Magazine's* "Best" readers awards.

6 ears of corn

Unsalted butter

Salt and freshly ground black pepper

1. Build a hot hardwood or charcoal fire or preheat a gas grill.

2. Place the unhusked corn on the hottest part of the grill and cook, turning a couple of times, until the husks begin to blacken, about 10 minutes. Move the corn to the slightly cooler edges of the grill (or reduce the heat) and continue to roast until the husks blacken and flake and the dimples of the kernels begin to show through the husks, 10 to 20 minutes longer. Younger, sweeter corn will take the shorter cooking time.

3. Pull down the top one-third of the husks before serving the corn with butter and salt and pepper.

6 servings

Bagaduce Lunch

Penobscot, Maine

This little gem of a clam shack on the Blue Hill peninsula is off the beaten path and somewhat tricky to locate, but it's well worth seeking out. You'll find the cheery white- and red-trimmed shack perched on a quiet knoll near a locally famous reversing falls on the Bagaduce River. A few red picnic tables overlook the quiet bay, where you can sit and watch the ospreys and bald eagles or simply soak up the serenity of this peaceful corner of Maine. Run by Judy and Mike Astbury and their

From Bagaduce Lun

CRABMEAT ROLL (PAGE 88)
DOUBLE-DIPPED ONION RINGS (PAGE 18
FRESH STRAWBERRY-RHUBARB PIE (PAGE 2

children, the third and fourth generations of the original founding family, Bagaduce Lunch has their formula down to a science. "We make everything ourselves," says Judy. "That way we can maintain our quality and keep it all under control." All seafood is local and impeccably fresh. Mike mans the fryer, turning out sweet whole-belly fried clams, Maine shrimp, scallops, and haddock, all served in rolls or as baskets. He hand- cuts the colossal onions for his famous onion rings and is also the coleslaw grinder, usually whipping up two batches a day. Judy does all the other salads, including one of the sweetest crabmeat salad rolls you've ever tasted and a delicious secret-recipe three-bean salad. Fried chicken and the usual hamburgers and hot dogs round out the menu. The dessert list is short and sweet: ice cream and pie — rich Maine-made Gifford's ice cream and, especially on weekends, locally made pies including strawberry-rhubarb, graham cracker cream, and blueberry and apple crumb.

Fresh-Squeezed Lemonade

Tidal Falls Lobster Restaurant in Hancock, Maine, has numerous claims to fame, including superb lobsters and a truly knockout view, but their amazingly delicious homemade lemonade might in and of itself be enough to get me there. Biggish slivers of lemon rind make all the difference.

8   **cups water**

1¼ **cups sugar**

1   **tablespoon coarsely shredded lemon zest, plus additional for garnish**

1½ **cups fresh lemon juice (about 1½ pounds, or 5 to 7 medium lemons)**

Thin lemon slices

Fresh mint

1. Heat 2 cups of the water in a medium saucepan. Add the sugar and stir until it dissolves. In a large pitcher, combine the sugar syrup with the remaining water, lemon zest, and lemon juice, stirring to blend well. Chill for at least 1 hour or until ready to serve.

2. Pour into tall glasses over ice, sprinkle with a little more lemon zest, and garnish with a thin lemon slice and a sprig of mint.

Makes about 9 cups

Coffin Family Coleslaw

Regis Coffin, one of the owners of Harraseeket Lunch and Lobster Company in the village of South Freeport, Maine, performs a multitude of the wide variety of tasks involved in running their large and busy operation, including making the daily batch of coleslaw. She shreds the cabbage — pounds and pounds of it every evening — in a special grinder that minces it up super-fine, then lets it sit overnight with some of its seasonings and dresses it in the morning. Crushed pineapple gives this coleslaw its sweet edge, making it the perfect foil for all manner of fried seafood.

1   **medium head green cabbage (about 1½ pounds), ground or finely shredded (about 9 cups)**

1   **can (8 ounces) crushed pineapple, undrained**

½   **cup cider vinegar**

6   **tablespoons sugar**

½   **cup Miracle Whip dressing, plus additional if necessary**

Salt and freshly ground black pepper

1. In a large bowl, toss the cabbage with the pineapple, vinegar, and sugar. Refrigerate, covered, for at least 4 hours or overnight.

2. Drain off any excess liquid. Add the Miracle Whip and stir thoroughly to combine. If the slaw does not seem moist enough, add a bit more dressing. Season to taste with salt and pepper. Use immediately or refrigerate for up to 4 hours. Spoon off any additional excess liquid before serving.

8 to 10 servings

COLESLAW HISTORY

"Coleslaw" derives its name from the Anglo-Saxon word for cabbage, *cal*, and the Dutch word *sla*, meaning salad. Dutch housewives in New York probably made the first coleslaw in this country, and it migrated up the New England coast from there.

Grandma's Pickled Beets

When Karen Flynn first opened The Bite on Martha's Vineyard, her Lithuanian grandmother told her she should add pickled beets to the menu because they were so good with fried fish. Karen was slightly skeptical at first, but she quickly realized how right Grandma was. The vinegary beets were a superb accompaniment to the seafood, and in fact she had to make more and more every week because they were always selling out! Here is Grandma Yankuns' recipe.

1   cup cider vinegar

1   can (1 pound) sliced cooked beets, drained

¼   cup sliced sweet white onion, such as Vidalia or Spanish

2   tablespoons vegetable oil

1. In a small saucepan, bring the vinegar to the boil. Put the beets in a mixing bowl and pour the hot vinegar over them. Add the onion; stir gently to combine.

2. Marinate the beets in the refrigerator for at least 8 hours or overnight.

3. Before serving, add the oil and stir to combine.

4 servings

Red Bliss Potato Salad

Barbara Flynn kindly shared this recipe for her famous dill-flecked Red Bliss Potato Salad. It's a mainstay on the menu at The Bite, her daughter Karen's clam shack in Menemsha on Martha's Vineyard, and Barbara makes pounds and pounds of it every week in the summer.

2½ **pounds unpeeled red-skinned potatoes, cut in 1½-inch chunks**

4 **tablespoons canola oil**

3 **tablespoons cider vinegar**

¼ **cup chopped sweet onion**

½ **cup mayonnaise, plus more if necessary**

½ **cup chopped fresh dill**

Salt and freshly ground black pepper

1. Bring a large pot of salted water to the boil. Cook the potatoes until tender, 15 to 20 minutes. Drain in a colander and let cool for 5 minutes.

2. Whisk the oil and vinegar together in a large bowl. Stir in the onion. Add the warm potatoes to the bowl. Mix with a large spoon or fork, breaking the potatoes up into smaller pieces and allowing the dressing to soak in. Stir in the mayonnaise and dill and season to taste with salt and pepper. Refrigerate for at least 1 hour or for up to 8 hours.

3. Before serving, taste for seasoning and add a bit more mayonnaise if the salad doesn't seem moist enough.

6 to 8 servings

FAMILY FISHERMEN

All summer long, Chuck Masso, owner of Chopmist Charlie's in Jamestown, Rhode Island, sneaks away on his boat whenever he can spare the time to go fishing. He finds that being out on the water in the early morning is the perfect antidote to the long (and often late) indoor hours required in the restaurant business — and, as a dividend, he can then present his customers with fish whose freshness he can personally vouch for. Chuck catches bluefish, fluke, flounder, sea bass, and striped bass ("stripers") and takes whatever he's caught that day right home to his dad, who is an expert fish filleter and has a big fillet table set up in the shade in his backyard. After they are removed from their frames, the fish are whisked right up to Chopmist. Lucky customers!

Up in Sedgwick, Maine, Bill Grant has been a lobsterman (they just call it "fishing" in Maine) all his adult life, and his son Patrick has chosen to follow in his father's footsteps.

"I can't put it any better than that well-known saying that goes 'A bad day fishin' sure beats a good day workin'," says Bill, with a grin.

That's ironic, of course, because there's no harder or riskier work than being a lobsterman — but he adds, "I could never work indoors all day. But what I really like is the independence. I don't like anybody telling me what I have to do."

Crusty Cracker-Dredged Onion Rings

Some cooks are reluctant to share their recipes, but when I asked Chris Butler what makes onion rings at Five Islands so especially tasty, he willingly gave up their formula — and it's a labor-intensive one. "We double dip 'em by hand, first in breading mix, then in cracker meal, with a dunk in egg white in between." These beauties emerge from the deep fryer with a nicely gnarled and deeply crunchy dark brown crust.

1 or 2 large onions, cut crosswise about ½-inch thick

1 cup breading mix (see Note)

2 egg whites

1 cup fine cracker meal (see Note)

½ teaspoon garlic powder

½ teaspoon coarse-ground black pepper

Vegetable oil for deep frying

Salt

1. Separate the onion into rings and soak in a large bowl of cold water for at least 1 hour. Place the breading mix, egg whites, and cracker meal mixed with garlic powder and pepper in three separate bowls.

2. Heat the oil in a deep fryer or deep pot to 350°F. Fill the fryer or pot no more than half full of oil.

3. Remove some of the onions from the water and dredge in the breading mix, shaking off the excess. Then dip into the egg whites and finally in the seasoned cracker meal, shaking off excess. If breading mixes get clumpy, shake rings in a colander. Slide into the hot oil. (Stand back; the moisture content may create spatter.) Cook, turning with tongs, until deep golden, 1 to 2 minutes.

4. Drain on paper towels, sprinkle with salt, and serve.

NOTE: Breading mix (see page 15) and cracker meal can be purchased in the breading section of the supermarket. If you can't find cracker meal, whir saltine crackers in a food processor until finely ground and smooth.

2 servings

Clam Box

Ipswich, Massachusetts

The Clam Box is shaped just like its name
— like a cardboard fried clam box — and sits jauntily along
Ipswich's Route 1A, in the heart of Massachusetts' North Shore
clam belt. Although the restaurant has been here for some 65
years, it came to regional renown in the 1970s, when then owner
Skip Atwood raised the bar of fried clam excellence — and all
other local establishments have been hustling to catch up ever
since. In the mid-1980s, Marina "Chickie" Aggelakis bought the
business from Skip. "Skip taught me everything I know," says
Chickie. "I haven't changed any of his ways of doing things —
just added a couple of items to the

From the Clam Box

FRIED CLAMS (PAGE 108)
AGGELAKIS TARTAR SAUCE (PAGE 187)
MY BEST GUESS AT CHICKIE'S COLESLAW (PAGE 190)

menu, like chowder and chicken fingers." Jane and Michael Stern call the Clam Box's fried clams the "the ultimate" on the North Shore, and since the North Shore is home of the best fried clams anywhere in the world, that is high praise indeed. And it's not just clams that are fried to perfection here. Longtime cook Dale Harrington, who insists on changing oil at least twice a day and maintains his fryers (which he has named Mabel and Louise) impeccably, turns out crisp, golden, meltingly tender, grease-free scallops, haddock, oysters, shrimp, and overflowing combo plat-ters of all of the above — plus onion rings and fries (from sepa-rate fryers called Phyllis, Dave, and Emily) — that are consistently, unbelievably good. All are accompanied by their homemade tartar sauce and a really special secret-recipe coleslaw. Plan on a wait in line at all but the most off hours, but it's well worth it — especially if Chickie happens to be passing out tastes of hot fried clams while you wait.

DESSERTS

Blueberry Cake

Brownies

Pies:
Blueberry
Berry Medley
Strawberry Rhubarb

Ice Cream
Chocolate
Strawberry
Vanilla
Almond Joy
Black Raspberry
Mint Chip

CHAPTER 9

Best of the Best Old-Fashioned Yankee Desserts

New Englanders have long been making wonderful desserts that are uniquely their own, many of them based on traditional English sweets such as custards and pies. Innovation and experimentation are all well and good, but there's also something immensely comforting in the kind of tradition and continuity that these classics represent. One could well assume that the likes of a homely, dark, molassesy Indian pudding might have vanished with the advent of the cult of the cutting edge, or that cinnamon-scented apple crisp or Grape-Nuts pudding, that idiosyncratic custardy New England specialty, might have gone the way of penny candy, but happily, they (and other scrumptious sweets like them) continue to show up on menus of the traditional eateries featured in this book. Nor have Yankees lost their taste for and skill at pie baking. Berries of all kinds, including the magnificent tart Maine wild blueberry, show up as fillings. Rhubarb is still a beloved favorite, and banana cream and other custard fillings are still consistently popular. More ice cream is consumed in New England than in any other region of the country, so it's no surprise that dairy bars (often doubling as clam shacks) sell tons and tons of their cold, sweet, delectable product every summer.

Banana Cream Pie

Plenty of places claim that their pies are "homemade" but neglect to mention that actually the crust is produced in a factory or that the custard filling is from a package. Not at Aunt Carrie's, where bakers arrive early, early every morning to roll out old-fashioned lard piecrust and to peel apples, hull strawberries, and chop rhubarb — and to cook bona fide, from-scratch, vanilla-flavored custard filling for their luscious banana cream pies. And whose recipe is it? Why, the bona fide Aunt Carrie's, of course! This is one of the many reasons why Aunt Carrie's won the coveted James Beard American Classic Award in 2007.

Crust

1	half recipe New England Lard Crust (page 206)

Filling

¾	cup sugar
½	cup all-purpose flour
3	tablespoons cornstarch
¾	teaspoon salt
½	cup whole milk
2	cups hot water
3	egg yolks
1	teaspoon vanilla extract
2	tablespoons butter
1	large or 2 small ripe bananas
½	cup heavy cream, whipped

1. Roll out the pastry on a lightly floured surface to a 12-inch round. Ease into a deep 9-inch pie plate. Trim the overhanging dough to ¾ inch all around. Turn the edges under, flush with the rim of the pie plate, and crimp or flute. Place the prepared shell in the freezer for at least 30 minutes.

2. Preheat the oven to 425°F. Bake the frozen pie shell until pale golden brown, 14 to 18 minutes. If the pastry starts to puff up, press the bottom gently with a large spoon or oven-mitted hand to flatten. Fill immediately or cool on a wire rack.

Continued on next page

3. For the filling, in a medium saucepan, whisk together the sugar, flour, cornstarch, and salt. Gradually whisk in the milk to make a smooth, thick paste. Whisk in the hot water. Place the saucepan over medium-high heat. Cook, whisking constantly, until the mixture comes to a boil, about 5 minutes. Remove from the heat.

4. In a small bowl, lightly whisk the egg yolks. Whisk about ½ cup of the hot custard mixture into the yolks. Return the yolk mixture to the saucepan and whisk until blended. Whisk in the vanilla and butter. Pour half of the hot custard into the prepared pie shell. Slice about two thirds of the banana (reserving the remaining third to decorate the top of the pie). Arrange the slices over the custard layer. Pour the remaining custard mixture over the bananas, smoothing the top. Cool completely in the refrigerator until the custard is set.

5. Whip the cream to medium-stiff peaks, spoon over the pie, and spread with a spatula. Refrigerate for at least 1 hour before serving. Decorate with sliced bananas just before serving.

6 to 8 servings

A FAMILY AFFAIR

Bagaduce Lunch on the Blue Hill peninsula is strictly a family affair. The business was started by Sid Snow in 1949, and Judy Astbury, Sid's granddaughter, has been working at the clam shack since the fourth grade. She and her husband, Mike, now run the business, and they're training their two daughters to take it over eventually. "I would hate for anyone else to have the business," said Judy. "It's always been in the family. That's the way it is, and I want it to stay that way."

New England Lard Crust

Lard, which is rendered and clarified pork fat, was the preferred and most available piecrust shortening for generations of New England bakers. Lard makes a meltingly tender piecrust, although this recipe also calls for a little butter to balance its distinctive, mildly nutty flavor.

2½ cups all-purpose flour

2 teaspoons granulated sugar

1 teaspoon salt

10 tablespoons chilled or frozen lard, cut in ½-inch chunks

2 tablespoons chilled unsalted butter, cut in ½-inch slices or chunks

6 to 8 tablespoons ice water

1. In the work bowl of a food processor, pulse the flour with the sugar and salt to blend. Distribute the lard and butter over the flour and pulse until most of the shortening is the size of small peas. Sprinkle 6 tablespoons of the water evenly over the flour mixture and pulse just until no dry flour remains and the dough begins to clump together into small balls. If the mixture is too dry to press into dough with your fingers, sprinkle on the remaining 1 to 2 tablespoons of water and pulse a few more times.

2. Turn out onto two sheets of plastic wrap, shape and flatten into 5-inch disks, and refrigerate for at least 1 hour or freeze. Remove the dough from the refrigerator 10 minutes before rolling it out. If frozen, thaw overnight in the refrigerator before using.

3. Roll pastry out to 11-inch rounds and use for two single-crust pies or one double-crust pie.

Makes two 9-inch single piecrusts

QUAHOG.ORG

Their slogan is "The definitive Rhode Island road trip." They describe their site as a guide to travel within the Ocean State, with a strong emphasis on food. Navigate around for great lists of clam shacks, diners, bakeries, creameries, and restaurants as well as explanations of such arcane Rhody-isms as N.Y. System hot dogs and cheese-less pizza strips. E-mail stuffie@quahog.org.

Indian Pudding

Indian pudding — so named because of the New England colonists' habit of terming anything made with corn "Indian" — is simply molasses-sweetened cornmeal mush baked into a pudding by the addition of eggs and milk. It's one of America's oldest desserts, and Aunt Carrie's has served it ever since the restaurant was founded in the 1920s. Elsie Foy, current co-owner and a direct descendant of the founding Aunt Carrie, agreed to give me the original recipe, which is a deliciously dark and sticky pudding that must be much like the one stirred up by those early English settlers.

3 ½ cups hot water

3 ½ cups whole milk

¾ cup yellow cornmeal

3 tablespoons butter

3 eggs

1 ¼ cups dark molasses

1 teaspoon salt

¾ teaspoon cinnamon

½ teaspoon ground ginger

Vanilla ice cream

1. Preheat the oven to 350°F. Lightly butter a 7- by 11-inch baking dish. In a large saucepan, combine the hot water and 2 cups of the milk. Whisk in the cornmeal. Place over low heat and cook, whisking every few minutes, until the mixture thickens to a thin, oatmeal-like consistency, 10 to 15 minutes. Remove from the heat and whisk in the butter.

2. Meanwhile, in a large bowl, lightly beat the eggs. Whisk in the molasses, salt, cinnamon, and ginger. Whisk the molasses mixture into the cornmeal mixture and pour into the prepared baking dish. Slowly pour the remaining 1 ½ cups of cold milk evenly over the top of the pudding batter. Bake for about 1 hour, or until a skin forms on top of the pudding and it is softly set. It will thicken considerably more as it cools.

3. Cool for at least 30 minutes, then serve. (Or cool completely. Rewarm in a microwave set on low power for about 5 minutes.) Serve with vanilla ice cream.

8 to 10 servings

Aunt Carrie's

Narragansett, Rhode Island

From Aunt Carrie's
BROILED FLOUNDER (PAGE 132)
BANANA CREAM PIE (PAGE 204)
NEW ENGLAND LARD CRUST (PAGE 206)
INDIAN PUDDING (PAGE 207)

If you ask anyone, anywhere in the state of Rhode Island about summertime shore eating, Aunt Carrie's tops everyone's list. For one thing, it's been in its divinely picturesque beach location since 1920, and it has been run by the same family, which is now into the fourth generation of descendants of the original (and very real) Aunt Carrie. You can still do takeout at their busy window and carry your order to your car or to the nearby beach, or you can step into the rambling old-fashioned dinner hall and thereby step back in time. This room has the look and feel of an early-twentieth-century family-style shore house, with a sloping old floor, screened double-hung windows, and cream-colored walls with green trim hung with old photographs depicting the evolution of the restaurant. The kitchen has hardly wavered since those early days, either, sticking by the beloved New England classics — with a uniquely Rhode Island twist, of course. This means that your chowder comes in three varieties — milk, tomato, or plain (plain meaning brothy) — and is

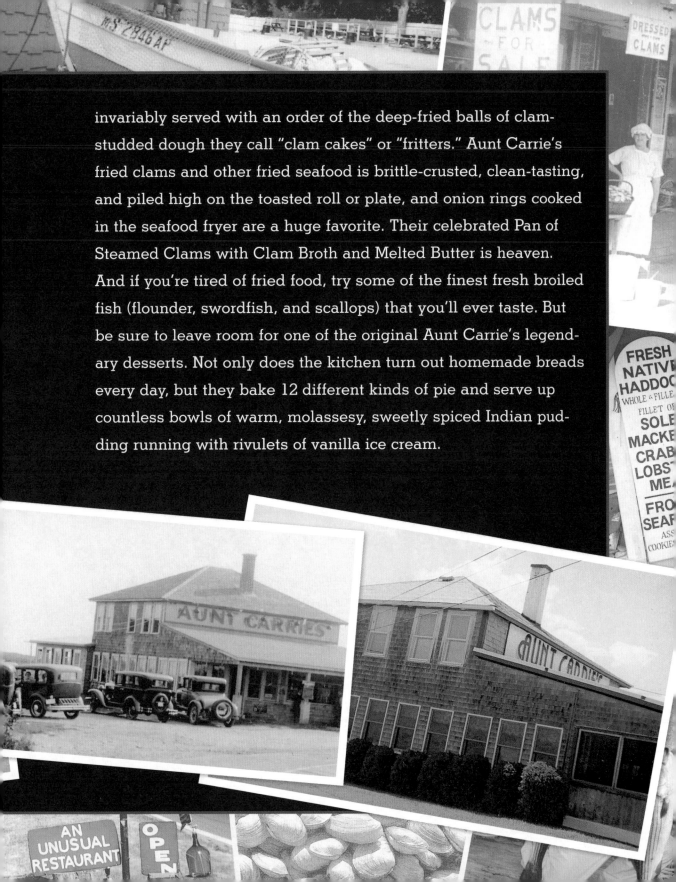

invariably served with an order of the deep-fried balls of clam-studded dough they call "clam cakes" or "fritters." Aunt Carrie's fried clams and other fried seafood is brittle-crusted, clean-tasting, and piled high on the toasted roll or plate, and onion rings cooked in the seafood fryer are a huge favorite. Their celebrated Pan of Steamed Clams with Clam Broth and Melted Butter is heaven. And if you're tired of fried food, try some of the finest fresh broiled fish (flounder, swordfish, and scallops) that you'll ever taste. But be sure to leave room for one of the original Aunt Carrie's legendary desserts. Not only does the kitchen turn out homemade breads every day, but they bake 12 different kinds of pie and serve up countless bowls of warm, molassesy, sweetly spiced Indian pudding running with rivulets of vanilla ice cream.

Orange Freeze

Captain Frosty's in Dennis, Massachusetts, features the complete gamut of ice cream desserts, including frappes (that's Cape Cod–ese for thick milk shakes), floats, hot fudge sundaes, and an over-the-top banana boat, but the Orange Freeze is the item most frequently ordered off their ice cream board. They make it with soft-serve ice cream, but a reasonable facsimile can be created at home with vanilla frozen yogurt or regular vanilla ice cream. It's the ideal refreshing pick-me-up to sip and savor after spending a day at a Cape Cod beach or in your own backyard.

1 **pint vanilla frozen yogurt or ice cream**

½ **cup thawed orange juice concentrate**

1. In a blender, combine the ice cream and orange juice concentrate. Whir until blended, smooth, and slightly frothy. Pour into one or two glasses.

2. Serve with a straw and a spoon.

1 large or 2 smaller servings

ICE CREAM DRINKS: NOMENCLATURE

What the rest of America knows as a "milk shake" (ice cream, milk, and syrup whipped up in a blender) is known as a "frappe" on Cape Cod and in other parts of coastal Massachusetts. Inland in the Bay State it's usually called a "frost." In parts of Rhode Island and South Coast Massachusetts, a frappe sometimes becomes a "cabinet" — and if you want a cabinet made with the locally popular sweet coffee syrup, you ask for a "coffee cab."

If you order a "milk shake" at a Massachusetts clam shack or ice cream stand, you're likely to be served a drink made with milk and flavored syrup, but without any ice cream whatsoever.

Grape-Nuts Pudding

Why you find Grape-Nuts pudding primarily in New England is a mystery to me, but this smooth custard pudding with its gently spiced nutty topping is one of those utterly delectable and soul-soothing comfort desserts that are a perfect finish to just about any supper. At Evelyn's in Tiverton, Rhode Island, owner Jane Bitto finds that her Grape-Nuts Pudding is so enduringly popular and in such constant demand that she must make it several times a week.

7	eggs
¾	cup sugar
2	cups whole or low-fat milk
1½	teaspoons vanilla extract
⅓	cup Post Grape-Nuts cereal
⅛	teaspoon ground cinnamon
⅛	teaspoon ground nutmeg

1. Preheat the oven to 350°F. Lightly butter a shallow 2-quart glass baking dish.

2. In a large bowl, whisk the eggs with the sugar. Whisk in the milk and vanilla. Pour this custard mixture into the prepared dish. Sprinkle the Grape-Nuts evenly over the top and sprinkle with cinnamon and nutmeg.

3. Place the pudding dish into a larger baking pan and fill the larger pan with boiling water to come about halfway up the sides of the pudding dish. Bake for 25 to 35 minutes, until the custard is softly set and a knife inserted in the center comes out clean. Do not overcook — the pudding will continue to cook a little bit after it comes out of the oven.

4. Cool on a wire rack for at least 30 minutes. Serve the pudding warm or lukewarm, or refrigerate and serve chilled.

6 to 8 servings

Granny Smith Apple Crisp

It was a blustery early-spring day when I first walked into Chopmist Charlie's in Jamestown, Rhode Island, and when I saw homemade apple crisp on the menu, I decided to try to order a meal that left plenty of room for dessert. That was no simple mission, what with needing to sample their rich lobster bisque, crisp swordfish nuggets, and bacon-studded Rhode Island stuffies (baked stuffed clams), but I persevered. The crisp was indeed homemade, warm and redolent of cinnamon and brown sugar, and was well worth leaving a little room for.

Oat Topping

½   cup regular or quick-cooking (not instant) rolled oats

¼   cup milk

4   tablespoons cold butter

¼   cup all-purpose flour

¼   cup brown sugar

2   tablespoons chopped walnuts, optional

Ingredients continue on next page

1. For the topping, in a small bowl, toss the oats with the milk. Set aside. In a large bowl, combine the butter, flour, and brown sugar. Use a pastry blender or two knives to cut the mixture together until it is crumbly and resembles coarse meal. Add the oats and the walnuts, if desired. Toss well to combine.

2. Preheat the oven to 350°F. Butter a 9-inch glass or ceramic baking dish.

Continued on next page

Apple Filling

6   Granny Smith apples, peeled, cored, and sliced ¼ inch thick

2   teaspoons lemon juice

1   cup water

¼   cup brown sugar

¼   cup granulated sugar

1   tablespoon arrowroot or cornstarch

1½ teaspoons cinnamon

¼   teaspoon salt

1   tablespoon apple schnapps or apple brandy

For Serving

Vanilla ice cream

3. In a bowl, combine the apples with the lemon juice and water to prevent them from browning. In a separate large bowl, combine the brown sugar, granulated sugar, arrowroot, cinnamon, and salt; mix well. Lift the apples out of their acidulated water and add to the sugar mixture, along with the apple schnapps. Mix together thoroughly and transfer to the prepared baking dish. The apples will be mounded in the dish but will sink as they bake. Sprinkle the topping mixture evenly over the apples.

4. Bake in the preheated oven until the filling is bubbly and the top is browned and crisp, 45 minutes to 1 hour. Cool for 30 minutes and serve warm, with vanilla ice cream.

6 servings

GRAY'S ICE CREAM

"I could make ice cream all day and all night," says Marilyn Dennis, owner of Gray's Ice Cream stand in Tiverton, Rhode Island. "It's my life."

In the summer, Marilyn and a battalion of teenage employees staff eight take-out windows, scooping out as much as a thousand gallons of homemade ice cream a day during a high-season weekend. The parking lot is jammed with happy people slurping and licking cones. Celebrities such as Kevin Bacon and Kyra Sedgwick have been spotted waiting in line along with everyone else. It doesn't faze Marilyn or impress her all that much. She trains her staff to treat everyone equally and to be nice to all. Anyway, Marilyn is usually too busy making ice cream out in the back to notice.

Cod End Cookhouse

Tenants Harbor, Maine

From Cod End

MEDITERRANEAN SEAFOOD STEW (PA...
GRILLED CHEESE SANDWICHES WITH
TOMATO (PAGE 82)
FISH CAKES (PAGE 166)
MAINE WILD BLUEBERRY PIE (PAGE 222)

This was the last stop on a three-day eating trip along midcoast Maine, and even though we'd put away more than our fair share of the best (and some of the worst) seafood in the state, Cod End's food was such a revelation that we somehow were hungry all over again. Anne Miller, the owner and prime mover behind Cod End, has maintained the very highest standards for 30 years, and they never waver. Housed in a charming old wooden building on a working fishing wharf, the cookhouse shares space with a retail fish market that showcases some of the best-looking fresh fish I've ever seen on ice. This is true in-the-rough eating, so after placing your order at a window, you take a seat at one of the inside picnic tables or out on the large deck, where you soak up a goodly dose of gorgeous Maine scenery while you wait. Every single thing we've ever eaten here has been wonderful, including a creamy thyme-flecked fish chowder, a dazzling, vegetable-filled Mediterranean sea-

food stew (perfect on a blustery day), fish cakes made with fresh hake and potato and seasoned with dill, sweet crabmeat, lobster, and shrimp rolls in butter-grilled buns, succulent whole-belly fried clams, and, for those times when you're seafooded out, an outstanding grilled Cheddar and tomato sandwich on anadama bread. Another menu plus: a really nice fresh garden salad made with mixed greens, fresh tomatoes, and homemade dressing. Plenty of people make their way to Cod End for the desserts alone. Anne Miller is famous for her blueberry cake, made from an old Matinicus Island recipe, and for her delectable pies (especially the berry ones), made with a melt-in-the-mouth homemade lard crust.

Fresh Strawberry-Rhubarb Pie

It's a tradition at Bagaduce Lunch to have homemade pie on the menu. Owner Judy Astbury's late mother, Vangie Peasley, made all the pies for years and years, and now that Vangie has passed on, another talented local pie maker has taken on the task. So you can still count on hand-crafted crust and fresh fillings such as this strawberry-rhubarb classic.

Vangie's Piecrust

2½ cups all-purpose flour

1 teaspoon salt

¾ cup solid vegetable shortening

6 to 8 tablespoons ice water

Ingredients continue on next page

1. For the crust, stir together the flour and salt in a large bowl. Cut the shortening into small pieces and add to the flour. Using a pastry blender, two table knives, or your fingertips, work the flour and shortening together until the shortening is the size of small peas. Sprinkle most of the ice water over the flour mixture and work the dough with a large fork or your hands, adding more water by tablespoons, until it is evenly moistened and begins to hold together. Divide into two balls, flatten into disks, wrap, and refrigerate for at least 30 minutes or for up to 2 days.

Continued on next page

Strawberry-Rhubarb Filling

2½ cups sliced rhubarb (about 1¼ pounds)

2½ cups hulled strawberries, halved or quartered if large (about 1½ pints)

1 cup sugar

2 tablespoons cornstarch

2 tablespoons butter

2. Remove the pastry from the refrigerator a few minutes before rolling out. Preheat the oven to 350°F. Roll out half the dough on a lightly floured surface to a 12-inch round. Ease into a 9-inch pie plate. Roll out the top crust.

3. In a bowl, toss the rhubarb, strawberries, sugar, and cornstarch to combine. Transfer to the pie shell. Cut the butter into small pieces and distribute over the fruit.

4. Cover with the top crust and trim the overhanging dough to ¾ inch all around. Turn the edges under and crimp or flute the edges to seal. Use a sharp knife to cut several vents in the crust.

5. Bake in the preheated oven until the crust is a rich golden brown and the fruit juices bubble through the vents, 45 to 60 minutes. Cool on a wire rack.

6 to 8 servings

Whoopie Pies

No one's quite sure of the origin of the name, but the mouthwatering, filling-oozing snack cake called the "whoopie pie" has become something of a Maine institution. Marshmallow cream filling sandwiched between two light cocoa sponge cakes forms a dessert that looks something like a chocolate burger. Whoopie pies are a frequently requested recipe at Harraseeket Lunch and Lobster in South Freeport, Maine, where they have been baking them for years. Whoopie pies are the perfect handheld dessert after one of Harraseeket's open-air lobster lunches or suppers.

Cakes

1	cup milk
1	teaspoon white vinegar
1½	teaspoons baking soda
½	cup solid vegetable shortening
1½	cups granulated sugar
½	cup unsweetened cocoa powder
2	eggs
2½	cups all-purpose flour
¾	teaspoon salt
1	teaspoon vanilla

Ingredients continue on next page

1. Preheat the oven to 350°F. Line two baking sheets with parchment paper.

2. For the cakes, in a small bowl, combine the milk and vinegar. Set aside for 10 minutes, until foamy and slightly thickened. Stir the baking soda into the milk mixture and let stand another 5 minutes.

3. In the large bowl of an electric mixer, cream together the shortening, sugar, and cocoa powder until blended. Add the eggs, and continue to beat until smooth.

4. In another large bowl, sift the flour with the salt. With the mixer on medium-low speed, add the flour to the shortening mixture by cupfuls, alternating with the milk; beat until fairly smooth. Beat in the vanilla.

5. Using a 2-ounce ice cream scoop or ¼-cup dry measure, scoop the batter onto the baking sheets, leaving at least 2 inches between each cake.

6. Bake in the preheated oven until the cakes are puffy, firm at the edges, and spring back when touched lightly on top, 12 to 15 minutes. Remove with a spatula to wire racks and cool completely. (The cakes can be made up to 2 weeks ahead and frozen.)

Continued on next page

Filling

¾ cup solid vegetable shortening

½ cup (1 stick) butter, softened

¾ cup Marshmallow Fluff (see Note)

1 pound powdered sugar

2 teaspoons vanilla

7. For the filling, cream together the vegetable shortening and butter in an electric mixer until well combined. Beat in the Marshmallow Fluff. With the mixer on low speed, add the powdered sugar. Increase the speed to high and beat until smooth and fluffy. Beat in the vanilla.

8. To assemble, spread the undersides of half the cakes with about ½ cup of filling and sandwich with another cake. The whoopee pies can be wrapped individually and stored at cool room temperature, in the refrigerator for up to 2 days, or frozen.

NOTE: To measure the Marshmallow Fluff, first grease the measuring cup with oil or vegetable oil spray.

10 to 12 whoopie pies

SCOOPER BOWL

Boston is known as the land of the bean and cod, but it should really be "bean, cod, and ice cream."

New Englanders love their ice cream, eating an average of something like 20 quarts per person annually versus the national average of 16 quarts. And in Boston, during early June every year, some 30,000 Scooper Bowl visitors consume more than 10 tons of ice cream and frozen yogurt, sampling close to 40 flavors from nine or so different companies. It's a chance for ice cream manufacturers to debut new flavors and get instant feedback — everything from tried-and-true chocolate and vanilla to such exotica as dinosaur crunch and lobster-flavored ice cream. (This event is held at City Hall Plaza, Boston.)

Harraseeket Lunch and Lobster Company

South Freeport, Maine

From Harraseeket Lunch

LOBSTER ROLL (PAGE 96)
COFFIN FAMILY COLESLAW (PAGE 195)
WHOOPIE PIES (PAGE 218)

Situated on a jetty in quiet, unspoiled South Freeport, Harraseeket Lunch is less than 5 miles from L.L. Bean and the outlet madness of Freeport, but it feels worlds away. This is a large and ambitious operation consisting of a take-out window, lots of picnic tables (many under awnings), and a lobster pound that sells live and boiled lobsters, steamers, corn, and new red potatoes. It takes at least five members of the Coffin

and Attiero families, along with a team of dedicated, mostly long-term employees, to run this amazingly efficient enterprise and to manage the summer crowds with good cheer. Harraseeket makes a lobster roll without peer, and their flavorful homemade chowders are rich and creamy and not overthickened. Batter-fried clams are something of a rarity in Maine, but Harraseeket is renowned for its buttermilk battered-fried whole-belly beauties, which emerge from the fryer hot, puffy, and golden. The oil gets changed at least once a day during high season, so all the fried seafood for that matter, including shrimp, scallops, fish, and crab-cakes (some of it breaded rather than battered) tastes especially fresh and sweet. And . . . the bonus here is Harraseeket's long list of incredible des-

serts, all homemade,
each one as good as
the next: cream pies
of all kinds (made
with Coffin family
recipes), strawberry
shortcake, bread pud-
ding, and one of the
best whoopie pies on
the Maine coast.

Maine Wild Blueberry Pie

Cod End Cookhouse owner Anne Miller's reputation as a premier pie maker precedes her up and down midcoast Maine — to the extent that other blueberry pies are judged as to whether they come close to the standard of an Anne Miller pie. It could be the handmade hot-water lard crust that has been passed down for several generations, it could be the juicy, unthickened wild Maine blueberry filling, or it could be all that, plus the care and love lavished on each pie she bakes.

Hot-Water Crust

12	tablespoons lard, cut into several chunks
¾	teaspoon salt
3	tablespoons boiling water
2	cups all-purpose flour

Blueberry Filling

5	cups blueberries, preferably wild Maine blueberries
¾	cup sugar, plus 1 tablespoon
¼	teaspoon cinnamon
⅛	teaspoon nutmeg
2	tablespoons butter

1. For the crust, combine the lard and salt in a large bowl. Pour the boiling water over and work the mixture with a large fork until the lard is softened and the salt is mixed in. Add the flour and, using a fork or your fingertips, work the mixture together until you can squeeze the dough into a cohesive mass. Divide in half and shape into two flattened disks. Wrap in plastic wrap and chill for at least 30 minutes or for up to 2 days.

2. Remove the pastry from the refrigerator 30 to 45 minutes before rolling out. Preheat the oven to 350°F. Roll half the dough out on a lightly floured surface to a 12-inch round. Ease into a 9-inch pie plate. Roll out the top crust.

3. Pour the blueberries into the pie shell. In a small bowl, toss together the sugar, cinnamon, and nutmeg. Reserve 1 tablespoon of the cinnamon sugar for sprinkling over the top crust. Sprinkle the remaining ¾ cup of cinnamon sugar over the berries, stirring gently to mix. Cut the butter into several pieces and distribute over the top.

4. Cover with the top crust and trim the overhanging dough to

Continued on next page

¾ inch all around. Turn the edges under, and crimp or flute the dough to seal. Use a sharp knife to cut several vents in the crust and sprinkle with the reserved tablespoon of cinnamon sugar.

5. Bake in the preheated oven until the crust is a rich golden brown and the berry juices bubble through the vents, about 45 minutes. Cool on a wire rack.

6 to 8 **servings**

MAINE'S BLUEBERRY FESTIVALS

To celebrate the state's wild blueberries, Maine puts on not one but two blueberry festivals every summer. The first is held in Machias, 75 miles northeast of Bar Harbor, on the third Friday and Saturday in August, and is called, simply, the Blueberry Festival. It's a thanksgiving for the blueberry harvest and a no-frills, down-home affair with a fish fry, an all-you-can-eat blueberry pancake break-fast, a wild blueberry dessert bar, and chowder and lobster. Events include a pie-eating contest, a blueberry baked goods contest, and presentation of a musical called "Red, White, and Blueberry."

Then there's the weeklong State of Maine Wild Blueberry Festival, held during the Union Fair at the fairgrounds during the last full week of August. (The Union fairgrounds are 14 miles northwest of Rockland.) Friday is official blueberry day, but blueberry events are scattered through the week. The "Blueberry Hut" is open all week, and there are coffee cake contests and blueberry pie–baking contests. Friday sees the big wild blueberry pancake breakfast, a pie-eating contest, and the coronation of the State of Maine Wild Blueberry Queen.

Sea Swirl

Mystic, Connecticut

From the Sea Sw

CORN CHOWDER (PAGE 70)
FRIED COD SANDWICH (PAGE 91)
OLD-FASHIONED ICE CREAM SODA
(PAGE 226)

Perched jauntily right on Route 1 in Mystic, the Sea Swirl looks like the Carvel stand it used to be, yet for its size, it offers a larger and more varied menu than many other clam shacks. In addition to spectacular fried seafood, fries, onion rings, burgers, and dogs, the Sea Swirl boasts home-made corn chowder and two types of clam chowder, appetizers

(such as deep-fried jalapeño poppers and broccoli and cheese florets), and homemade chili. Like all the best clam shacks, it draws a wonderfully diverse crowd, too, with nattily clad businessmen and neat tourists lining up alongside barefoot kids in bathing suits and construction workers. There's no water view, but some of the picnic tables face the tidal marsh behind the restaurant. For almost 25 years, Sea Swirl has been a husband-and-wife operation, and owners Dave and Kathleen Blaney are sticklers for quality, using fresh cod, scallops, and lobsters that Dave picks up daily from

the Stonington docks. They fry in premium oil in a top-quality fryer that filters the oil constantly. A wedge of pristine, ocean-sweet fried cod spills out over the sides of a toasted bun, fried shrimp are lightly battered and crisp, and scallops are succulent. And, in keeping with its origins, the Sea Swirl offers a full menu of soft-serve and premium hard ice cream cones, drinks, and sundaes, including a slurping-good old-fashioned ice cream soda that is absolute perfection on a hot summer day.

Old-Fashioned Ice Cream Soda

The Sea Swirl clam shack in Mystic, Connecticut, started life as a Carvel stand many years ago, so it seems absolutely appropriate that they still serve the full roster of ice cream desserts and drinks, both soft-serve and regular. Here is their formula for the classic ice cream soda. When this is made with vanilla ice cream, it's called a "black-and-white."

⅓ cup chocolate syrup

¼ cup half-and-half

About 12 ounces seltzer
    water

2 scoops ice cream
   — vanilla, chocolate,
   and coffee are favorites

1. In a tall glass, stir together the chocolate syrup and half-and-half to mix well. Fill with seltzer water to about two-thirds full. Add the ice cream. Finish with enough additional seltzer to fill the glass to the brim, stirring gently to create some frothy bubbles on top.

2. Serve with a long spoon and straw.

1 serving

PORTUGUESE BAKERY

The Portuguese Bakery at 299 Commercial Street in Provincetown on Cape Cod is a must-stop for a fortifying snack so that you can continue the endless people-watching stroll that is probably Provincetown's main attraction. This old-fashioned bakery sells tasty goodies galore, including sweet Portuguese breads; *malassadas*, which are like deep-fried crullers rolled in granulated sugar; *rabanada*, akin to portable French toast; and tiny custard tarts. You can also pick up great Portuguese sandwiches, such as chourico and peppers, for a quick walk-away lunch.

Portuguese Bread Pudding

Jerry Carreiro, chef-owner of Tip For Tops'n in Provincetown, Massachusetts, makes big batches of this Portuguese bread pudding from his grandmother's recipe every week. Portuguese bread has a firm, chewy texture and a well-browned crust, and it is similar enough to Italian bread that the latter could easily be substituted. I like this bread pudding best served warm, topped with a small scoop of vanilla ice cream and, in summer, an additional scattering of fresh berries.

4	eggs
1	cup sugar
4	cups whole milk
1½	teaspoons vanilla extract
½	teaspoon cinnamon
¼	teaspoon nutmeg
½	cup raisins
3	tablespoons softened butter
8	ounces sliced Portuguese or Italian bread
3	tablespoons butter, melted

Vanilla ice cream

1. In a large bowl, whisk together the eggs and sugar. Whisk in the milk, vanilla, cinnamon, and nutmeg. Stir in the raisins. Generously butter the bread with the softened butter. Submerge the bread in the egg mixture and set aside for at least 20 minutes. Use your hands or a large spoon to break the soaked bread into smaller chunks.

2. Preheat the oven to 350°F. Generously butter a 9- by 11-inch glass baking dish.

3. Transfer the soaked bread to the baking dish and smooth the top. Drizzle with the melted butter.

4. Bake in the preheated oven until the top of the pudding puffs and browns and a knife inserted in the center comes out clean, 50 minutes to 1 hour. Serve warm or at room temperature topped with the vanilla ice cream.

6 to 8 servings

Blueberry-Raspberry Squares

They bake several batches of delectably buttery, chewy squares every day in the summer at the Tidal Falls Lobster Restaurant in Hancock, Maine. For most of the season, they use just blueberries, but during the few brief weeks that fresh raspberries are being picked locally, they add both berries. It's a versatile dessert — wonderful served on a plate, topped with a cloud of whipped cream or a scoop of vanilla ice cream, or as the perfect handheld finish to one of Tidal Falls' glorious lobster feasts.

Dough

1½ cups all-purpose flour

1½ cups sugar

10 tablespoons butter, melted

2 eggs, lightly beaten

1 cup fresh or frozen blueberries

1 cup fresh raspberries

Topping

2 tablespoons sugar

2 teaspoons cinnamon

For Serving

Whipped cream or vanilla ice cream, optional

1. Preheat the oven to 350°F. Butter a 9- by 13-inch glass baking dish.

2. In a large bowl, combine the flour and sugar and mix well. Drizzle with the melted butter, add the eggs, and use a wooden spoon to blend well. Sprinkle the blueberries and raspberries onto the dough and fold them in gently but thoroughly, trying not to crush the berries too much. Scrape into the prepared baking dish and use a spatula or the clean palm of your hand to spread the dough out more or less evenly.

3. To make the topping, in a small bowl, combine the sugar and the cinnamon.

4. Bake in the preheated oven until lightly browned and firm to the touch in the center, 45 to 50 minutes. Five minutes before the end of the baking time, sprinkle the top evenly with the cinnamon sugar.

5. Cool on a wire rack until lukewarm and cut into 12 squares. Serve as a dessert, topped with whipped cream or ice cream, if desired, or eat out of hand.

Makes 12 large squares

Oatmeal Pie

At Two Lights Lobster Shack in Cape Elizabeth, Maine, they've been making this scrumptious pie since 1968 — and to much local acclaim. It's an unusual dessert, similar to a pecan pie, but not as sweet or rich. Rolled oats contribute an elusive nutty flavor (though you'd never guess they were in there!), and the shredded coconut adds its own unique texture and richness.

2   large eggs

¾   cup whole milk

4   tablespoons melted butter

1½   teaspoons vanilla extract

½   cup shredded sweetened coconut

½   cup granulated sugar

¾   cup light corn syrup

¾   cup quick-cooking (not instant) rolled oats

1   nine-inch pie shell

Whipped cream, optional

1. Preheat the oven to 350°F.

2. In a large bowl, lightly whisk the eggs just until smooth. Whisk in the milk, melted butter, vanilla, coconut, sugar, and corn syrup. Stir in the rolled oats. Pour the mixture into the pie shell.

3. Bake in the preheated oven until the filling is no longer wobbly in the center and the top is light golden brown, about 40 minutes.

4. Cool the pie on a wire rack before cutting into wedges. Serve with a dollop of whipped cream, if desired.

6 to 8 servings

Bristol, Rhode Island, and Environs

Water, water everywhere you look, and good eating almost everywhere you stop — two hallmarks of the Ocean State. Newport is certainly well worth a visit, but for a more authentically Rhode Island experience I'd suggest a weekend based in Bristol, with food forays out from there. Bristol is a beautiful town with a rich history and it's situated right on Narragansett Bay. After unpacking, first stroll the accessible few-block downtown and check out the fascinating architectural blend — an evolving mix of original and rehabbed old buildings. Then . . .

FRIDAY NIGHT

Walk, bike-ride, or drive to **Quito's Restaurant** (page 168) on the harbor and sit indoors or out on the patio under the twinkling clam shell lights. You've got your choice of classic New England fare (fried seafood, steamers, etc.) or Italian-influenced specialties such as clams with oil and garlic or Seafood Mediterranean.

SATURDAY MORNING

Breakfast at your B & B (there are many in and around town) or take a stool at the formica counter at the tiny **Hope Diner**, a great little greasy spoon (meant as a compliment). Their catchy motto: "Don't be a dope, eat at the Hope!" Everything is good here, but I'm especially partial to the "O'Doris" which is fried egg over an English muffin with bacon or sausage all served up with hand-cut home fries studded with shards of blackened onion.

SATURDAY NOON

Include Tiverton in your road trip (which might take in the entire lovely area around Route 77) so you don't miss the **Evelyn's Drive-In** experience (see page 26). Claim a covered picnic table beside beautiful Nanaquaket Pond and feast on clam cakes, chowder, stuffies, or fried seafood. Share an order of their creamy Grape-Nuts pudding for dessert.

ICE CREAM BREAK

After more touring, stop back in Tiverton for a **Gray's Ice Cream** cone (see page 213) — thirty flavors, hand-churned, award-winning, and a Rhode Island institution. Gray's also has a branch on the dock in Bristol.

SATURDAY DINNER

Drive over the Mt. Hope bridge. If you're up for a slightly raucous beachy scene, check out the legendary **Flo's** (see page 100) in Middletown. (Hint: A good spot from which to observe the passing parade is their Topside Bar). Or cross yet another bridge over to Jamestown for a wonderful seafood meal at the convivial **Chopmist Charlie's** (see page 18). For a special splurge, reserve a table and head in the other direction to **The Back Eddy** (see The Ultimate Stuffie, page 16) in Westport Point, Massachusetts.

SUNDAY

If time permits, cross a few more bridges and explore the western shore of the bay in and around Narragansett. There's a lot of good eating here, including **Aunt Carrie's** (see page 208), a classic Rhode Island shore hall, and **Champlin's** (see page 126) overlooking the ferry slip on Galilee Harbor. Be sure to make a stop at **Iggy's** (see page 237) for a grease-spotted bag of doughboys.

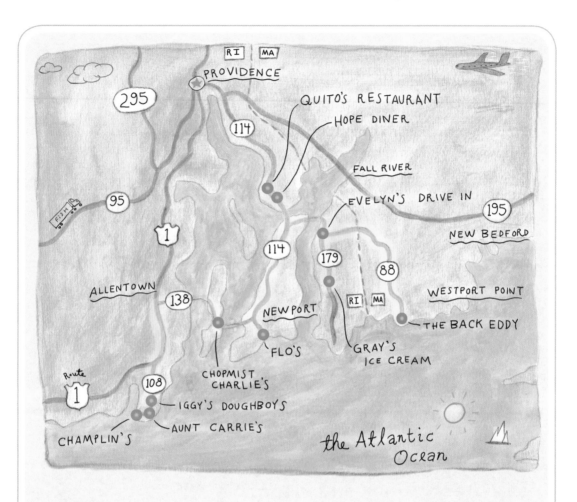

SPLURGE

The Back Eddy, right on Horseneck Beach in Westport Point, Massachusetts, is like the ultimate upscale clam shack. Inside the rooms are airy and spacious, and a large outdoor patio/bar leads down to a dock. (You can arrive by boat, too, and tie up overnight.) The wait staff is young, professional, and cheery, and the whole place has the good-times vibe of a stylish but casual party. And the food is fabulous.

Founder Chris Schlesinger sold to former manager Sal Liotta a couple of years ago, but the menu hasn't changed much. It still reflects Chris's punched-up takes on Yankee and Portuguese–New England classics, as well as a few Asian- and Mediterranean-influenced dishes. The emphasis is on cooking with produce from local farmers, seafood caught by local fishermen, and wine, beer, and cheese from local artisan producers. Whatever else you get, you must include an order of Back Eddy Stuffed Clams (see The Ultimate Stuffie, page 16), an inspired version of the classic. Other great starters are their sea clam and roasted corn chowder and the Thai-style mussels. Applewood bacon-wrapped giant New Bedford scallops with succotash are wonderful, as is the oven-roasted native cod loin with local clams, Portuguese sausage, and green olives, and the classic fish and chips with hand-cut fries and Eddy slaw. Reservations needed. (See Resources, page 240.)

Portland In the Rough

Portlanders love to say that Portland has more restaurants per capita than any other city in the country, except San Francisco. Whether or not that's true, you surely won't go hungry here (see Splurge, page 232), and you can also still find lots of simply cooked fresh seafood and a bona fide Maine experience. Commercial Street, which runs along the harbor in the city's Old Port, is a funky blend of touristy and the real deal. Poke around on the wharves — the buildings are a mix of falling-down shanties and gentrified brick warehouses and condos — and you'll feel like you've stepped back a century or so. There's fishing gear, draped bait-smelly nets, a catch being off-loaded on the old cobbled alleys, and a few stray cats.

FRIDAY NIGHT

One of those alleys is home to **J's Oyster Bar** (see page 58) and there's no better place to unwind than in this saloon-cum-restaurant. Something of an undiscovered gem, J's draws a genial crowd of local businessmen and fishermen. Slurp some iced oysters or clams from the raw bar or order any of their fabulous seafood dishes and enjoy some great people-watching.

SATURDAY MORNING

Staying within the Old Port, walk down Commercial Street to **Becky's Diner**, a local hangout (also discovered by the tourists) serving straightforward breakfast food. Salty waitresses dish it out, along with one-liners and folk wisdom.

SATURDAY NOON

If you've trekked up to Freeport to visit the venerable Mr. L.L. Bean, by now you're overdue for a break. Head straight for **Harraseeket Lunch and Lobster** (page 220). It's just a few miles away down a narrow neck in South Freeport, but this peaceful village is a

welcome contrast to the shopping frenzy. Order at the window for their batter-dipped clams, fantastic lobster rolls and onion rings, or on the back porch for boiled just-caught lobster. Take away one of their famous whoopee pies for gooey car snacks.

ICE CREAM BREAK

Back in the Old Port, get a big scoop of delectable toasted coconut organic ice cream at **Maple's Organics** on Middle Street. Or, just a few miles south off the turnpike is **Smiling Hill Farm** in Westbrook. Their dairy store sells hand-packed cones, sundaes, frappes, or floats.

SATURDAY DINNER

Depends on your mood and whether you crave more lobster. If you do, then **Two Lights Lobster Shack** (page 120) is just the ticket. It's south of the city, perched on a rocky headland, and it dispenses great steamed lobster, lobster rolls, and all manner of terrific fried seafood. Or, for another type of experience altogether, make a reservation at the world-class **Fore Street Restaurant** (see Splurge).

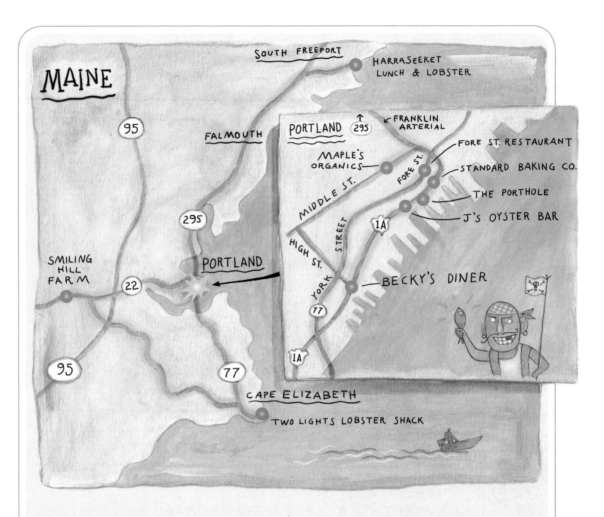

SUNDAY MORNING

One of the best bakeries in all of New England is the **Standard Baking Company** in the Old Port. Have a cup of their excellent coffee, nibble an incomparable sticky bun, and linger over the newspaper. At the other end of the spectrum is **The Porthole**, a charming gritty hole in the wall where you can get a beer or a little hair of the dog to wash down your eggs and toast.

SPLURGE

Sam Hayward has received tons of well-deserved accolades for his restaurant, **Fore Street**. He was one of the first chefs on the East Coast to extol the use of local ingredients, and his commitment to buying only local produce, seafood, and other products remains firm. The restaurant is housed in a handsomely rehabbed brick industrial building and much of the food — the menu changes daily — is cooked on a dramatic 17-foot open hearth so the bouquet of wood smoke perfumes the air. I have never had a less-than-wonderful dish here — from iced Pemaquid oysters or gratin of slacked salmon or lobster tart or wood-oven roasted mussels, to charred hangar steak or local scallops grilled over Maine applewood or two-texture duck, or spit-roasted pork loin. A local cheese platter is my choice for dessert, but other options can include warm chocolate soufflé cake or fruit tarte tatins. The wine list is world class, too. Reservations are a must. (See Resources, page 240.)

A Clam Alley Crawl

The area north and east of Boston known as the North Shore encompasses Cape Ann (Gloucester and Rockport) and other such historic towns as Salem and Marblehead. Clam shack connoisseurs know this piece of real estate as Clam Alley, and fabled Route 133, which runs from Ipswich, through Essex, and then into Gloucester, is sometimes called the Clam Superhighway. Some of the clam shacks along this route have become super-famous, but they're mostly still housed in their original ramshackle buildings, they still dish out jokes and brash good humor, and they still don't take themselves too seriously.

Clams, though — they're still serious about clams.

Here's what a couple of days spent on the North Shore might look like.

FRIDAY NIGHT ARRIVAL

Score a seat at one of the picnic tables at **Woodman's** (page 38) the granddaddy of all clam shacks, or, if the weather is fine, pick up some cold beer or wine and head out to the deck at **The Lobster Pool** on Folly Cove (page 237) outside Rockport. Order up a big bucket of steamers and join the crowd applauding as the sun sinks behind Plum Island.

SATURDAY MORNING

Gloucester is a fishing town, and fishermen are up early and serious about breakfast. Eat with the locals at one of several good spots — **Two Sisters**, **Lee's**, or **The Dory** — get stacks of pancakes, eggs and Portuguese sausage, or house-made muffins, and soak up the flavor of this venerable old town.

SATURDAY NOON

If you haven't had any yet, it's high time for some fried clams! Get in line at the **Clam Box** (look for the building shaped like . . . a clam box) in Ipswich (page 200) or scarf down some almost equally scrumptious whole-bellies at **J. T. Farnham's** (page 176) on the marsh in Essex. You could hit both places for a comparison test.

ICE CREAM BREAK

Stop at **White Farms Ice Cream** — at the sign of the giant cow in Ipswich near Crane's Beach — for lighter-than-usual handmade ice cream. Two flavors popular with the locals are Frozen Pudding (kind of like rum-raisin but more fruit) and Grape-Nuts.

SATURDAY DINNER

Two great options for a sit-down meal: Gloucester's **Causeway Restaurant** (page 236) for fabulous seafood with some Italian tweaks — very informal, always crowded, always fun, or make a reservation at the sweet (and more tranquil) family-run **Village Restaurant** in Essex (see page 237), where you can sit outdoors or in. Save room for the Indian pudding.

SUNDAY

Have a light breakfast and spend the day swimming or walking at Crane Beach in Ipswich or imbibing local history at the Essex Shipbuilding Museum. Other options are a stroll through Marblehead's historic Old Town or a visit to Gloucester's waterfront, where you can book a boat charter or a whale watching tour. Between activities, get in line at one of the shacks to beat the crowds for more fried clams.

More Stops Along the Way . . .

CONNECTICUT

Abbott's Lobster in the Rough
117 Pearl Street, Noank, CT
860-536-771
www.abbotts-lobster.com
Tuck into a steamed lobster or hot buttered lobster roll at this sprawling vintage lobster shack overlooking Long Island Sound and the Mystic River. Nothing fried here.

Costello's Clam Shack
145 Pearl Street, Noank, CT
860-572-2779
www.costellosclamshack.com.
Abbott's sister restaurant just up the street, but here almost everything is fried, including whole-belly clams, clam fritters, and cod.

Cove Fish Market
20 Old Stonington Road, Mystic, CT
860-536-0061
www.covefishmarket.com
It's still a fish market but you can also sit at a picnic table and savor a cup of their award-winning clear clam chowder or a lobster roll.

Flanders Fish Market and Restaurant
22 Chesterfield Road (Route 161),
East Lyme, CT
860-739-8866
http://flandersfish.com
Located inland on an unprepossessing commercial stretch, "FFM" attracts devoted followers in search of super-fresh seafood. Their fish and chips is a winner.

Johnny Ad's
910 Boston Post Road,
Old Saybrook, CT
860-388-4032
http://johnnyads.com
There's a pleasantly retro '50s feel in this modest spot on Route 1, and they still make their whole-belly clams and lobster rolls (chilled or hot buttered — the same way they have since Johnny opened the place in 1957.

Lenny's Indian Head Inn
205 South Montowese Street,
Branford, CT
203-488-1500
www.lennysnow.com
Slip into a wooden booth or dine marshside on the patio. Good bets are chowder (choice of creamy or clear), clams or oysters on the half shell, and — in a nod to Connecticut's Italian influence — their garlicky zuppa d'clams.

Overton's Seafood
80 Seaview Avenue, East Norwalk, CT
www.overtons-seafood.com
Too many clam shacks in southern Connecticut have given way to condos, but this tiny spot right on the Norwalk harbor holds on. Get your fried seafood at the window and carry it up to the covered rooftop deck to watch the goings-on.

MAINE

Barnacle Billy's
50-70 Perkins Cove Road,
Ogunquit, ME
800-866-5575
www.barnbilly.com
Still going strong after more than 45 years, this place has expanded into a fairly commercial operation but you can still get superb Maine lobster — steamed, stewed, or stuffed in a roll.

Beals' Lobster Pier
182 Clark Point Road, Southwest Harbor (Mount Desert Island), ME
800-245-7178
www.bealslobster.com
Located on the large working pier overlooking a famous Mount Desert harbor, this classic summer-only establishment offers both steamed lobster and some fried seafood as well.

Bob's Clam Hut
315 Route 1, Kittery, ME
207-439-4233
www.bobsclamhut.com
Kittery has grown up around this place but Bob still serves up some of the best fried seafood in southern Maine.

Boothbay Lobster Wharf
90 Atlantic Avenue,
Boothbay Harbor, ME
800-996-1740
www.boothbaylobsterwharf.com
Around the bend from the busiest part of Boothbay, this lobster pound delivers no-frills lobster dinners served at picnic tables.

Chauncey Creek Lobster Pier
16 Chauncey Creek Road,
Kittery Point, ME
207-439-1030
www.chaunceycreek.com
Just across the border into Maine, this sprawling lobster dock is situated on a tree-shrouded estuary. It's mostly lobster but offers a few fried seafood items as well.

Dennett's Wharf Restaurant and Oyster Bar
15 Sea Street, Castine, ME
207-326-9045
www.dennettswharf.net
Eat on the wharf and watch luxury yachts and work boats while enjoying fried seafood and seafood rolls in this full-service restaurant.

Fisherman's Friend Restaurant
5 Atlantic Avenue, Stonington, ME
207-367-2442
www.fishermansfriendrestaurant.com
A full-service seafood establishment that delivers wonderful chowder, fried seafood, and lobster in fascinating Stonington, which some consider the lobster capital of Maine.

Miller's Lobster Company
83 Eagle Quarry Road,
Spruce Head, ME
207-594-7406
www.millerslobster.com
It's lobster-in-the-rough at this scenic spot on a wharf surrounded on three sides by water.

Red's Eats
Route 1, Wiscasset, ME
207-882-6128
Some claim it to be the best lobster roll in Maine — the meat from a whole lobster in every butter-toasted bun — but the crowds can make scoring one daunting.

Susan's Fish and Chips
1135 Forest Avenue, Portland, ME
207-878-3240
http://susansfishnchips.com
Consistently good seafood fried to order and cheerfully served up in a bare-bones converted garage space in a neighborhood outside the busy Old Port.

Trenton Bridge Lobster Pound
Route 3, Trenton, ME
207-667-2977
www.trentonbridgelobster.com
The oak-fired pots are always steaming at this popular pound right on Route 3 at the bridge over to Mount Desert Island.

Waterman's Beach Lobster
343 Waterman's Beach Road,
South Thomaston, ME
207-596-7819
www.watermansbeachlobster.com
Just-caught lobsters are steamed over sea water at this straightforward and reliable James Beard American Regional Classic award-winner.

Young's Lobster Pound
4 Mitchell Street, Belfast, ME
207-338-1160
This is a true pound, with huge tanks holding thousands of lobsters inside the large red building. Choose your very own, have it steamed, and sit on the deck overlooking Belfast Bay to pick it apart.

MASSACHUSETTS

Arnold's Lobster & Clam Bar
3580 Route 6, Eastham, MA
508-255-2575
http://arnoldsrestaurant.com
The lines can be long but they move quickly, and the fried seafood here — especially the clams — make it worth the wait.

Causeway Restaurant
76 Essex Avenue, Gloucester, MA
978-281-5256
Huge portions of fresh seafood cooked with an Italian accent are the hallmarks at this convivial, always-crowded establishment.

The Clam Shack
277 Clinton Avenue, Falmouth, MA
508-540-7758
Order fried whole-belly clams or clam strips, a lobster roll, and onion rings and eat on the dock overlooking Falmouth Harbor.

Handy Hill Creamery
55 Hix Bridge Road, Westport, MA
508-636-8888
The place isn't on the water but stop on your way to or from the beach to pick up a fried seafood roll, a stuffie, or a hand-dipped cone.

Kelly's Roast Beef
410 Revere Beach Boulevard, Revere, MA
781-284-9129
www.kellysroastbeef.com
Juicy roast beef sandwiches for sure at this Revere institution, but also great fried seafood — especially the scallops. Four other locations around Boston, but the original is here in Revere

Kream 'N' Kone
961 Main Street, (Route 28), West Dennis, MA
508-394-0808
www.kreamnkone.com
Eat inside or out and enjoy the fried clams (whole belly or strips), scallops, or shrimp — and a soft-serve ice cream cone for dessert.

Larsen's Fish Market
56 Basin Road, Menemsha, MA
508-645-2680
www.larsensfishmarket.com
Whereas The Bite (page 186) does only fried seafood, Larsen's has the lobster and a raw bar concession in Menemsha. It's a long-standing agreement between the two places, so . . . it just depends on your mood!

The Lobster Pool
329 Granite Street (Route 127), Rockport, MA
978-546-7808
www.lobsterpoolrestaurant.com
Try to score a seat on the deck — especially dramatic as the sun sets over Ipswich Bay — and order up some chowder and steamers from the self-service window. Good desserts, too.

Mac's Seafood
265 Commercial Street, Wellfleet, MA
508-349-0404
www.macsseafood.com
Skip the sushi and grilled scallop burrito and order local oysters-on-the-half-shell, lobsters, or fried seafood at this popular small spot right on Wellfleet's working harbor.

Union Oyster House
41 Union Street, Boston, MA
617-227-2750
www.unionoysterhouse.com
Come for a bowl of chowder and a taste of history at this vintage establishment near Boston Harbor. It claims to be the oldest continuously operating restaurant in the country.

Village Restaurant
55 Main Street (Route 133), Essex, MA
978-768-6400
http://wedigclams.com
Another option on the Clam Superhighway, offering sit-down lunch or dinner with seating indoors or out. Famous for delicately crispy lard-fried clams, lobster pie, and rich baked haddock.

Way Back Eddy
1 Bridge Road at Horseneck Beach, Westport, MA
508-636-6500
www.thebackeddy.com
A laid-back spinoff of the famous Back Eddy restaurant across the street, this beachy shack serves a great fried fish sandwich.

NEW HAMPSHIRE

Brown's Lobster Pound
407 Route 286, Seabrook Beach, NH
603-474-3331
www.brownslobsterpound.com
Steamers and lobsters by the pound and cooked to order are the mainstays at this old-fashioned shore hall, but you can also get good fried seafood.

Newick's
431 Dover Point Road, Dover, NH
603-742-3205
www.newicks.com
Newick's is a New Hampshire institution, famous for its award-winning chowder and fried fisherman's platter — or try the buttery crumb-topped scallop or lobster pie.

Petey's Summertime Seafood
1323 Ocean Boulevard (Route 1A), Rye, NH
603-433-1937
www.peteys.com
Stop by the sometimes rowdy indoor-outdoor upstairs deck and enjoy fried seafood or a bowl of their legendary mixed seafood chowder.

RHODE ISLAND

Anthony's Seafood
963 Aquidneck Avenue, Middletown, RI
401-848-5058
www.anthonysseafood.net
Skip the fancified stuff on the menu and opt for a spicy stuffie and that good old-fashioned Rhode Island duo, "chowder and cakes" — brothy chowder and fried clam cakes for dipping.

The Black Pearl
Bannister's Wharf, Newport, RI
401-846-5264
www.blackpearlnewport.com
Okay, it's more upmarket than our usual picks, but this large, casually spiffy restaurant is Newport's best bet for reliably good seafood — plus great people-watching.

Cap'n Jack's
706 Succotash Road, Wakefield, RI
401-789-4556
www.capnjacksrestaurant.com
This rambling full-service establishment has an extensive menu, but we recommend their fried fisherman's platter, lobster roll with fries, and clam cakes.

George's of Galilee
250 Sand Hill Cove Road, Narragansett, RI
401-783-2306
www.georgesofgalilee.com
It's a 60-year-old institution with a lively bar scene and famous for its clam cakes (upward of 12,000 fried per day) and stuffies.

Horton's Seafood
809 Broadway, East Providence, RI
401-434-3116
http://hortonsseafood.com
Established in 1945, Horton's serves good versions of Rhode Island shack fare such as stuffies, snail salad, chowder (clear, white, or red), and cakes.

Iggy's Doughboys & Chowder House
889 Oakland Beach Avenue, Warwick, RI
401-737-9459
www.iggysdoughboys.com
It's a dependable source for chowder and clam cakes and fried calamari, but Iggy's is best known for their doughboys, puffed, sugar-dredged squares of fried dough. (Also with a Narragansett location.)

Starboard Galley
5 Angell Road, Narragansett, RI
401-782-1366
www.starboardgalleyrestaurant.com
Relocated from Narragansett, this take-out joint lays claim to having "The Best Clamcakes and Chowda Anywhere."

Geographic Listing of Profiled Clam Shacks, Lobster Pounds, and Chowder Houses

Connecticut

Lenny & Joe's Fish Tale, 86 Boston Post Road (Route 1), Westbrook, CT 06498. 860-669-0767.
http://ljfishtale.com

The Place Restaurant, 901 Boston Post Road (Route 1), Guilford, CT 06437. 203-453-9276.
http://theplaceguilford.com

Seahorse Restaurant, (formerly the Seahorse Tavern) 65 Marsh Road, Noank, CT 06340. 860-415-4280.
http://seahorserestaurant.net

Sea Swirl, Junction of Route 1 and Route 27, Mystic, CT 06355. 860-536-3452.
www.seaswirlofmystic.com

Maine

Running from south to north — or east — up the coast

Maine Diner, 2265 Post Road, (Route 1), Wells, ME 04090. 207-646-4441.
www.mainediner.com

The Clam Shack, Route 9 at the Kennebunkport Bridge, Kennebunkport, ME 04046. 207-967-3321.
http://theclamshack.net

Two Lights Lobster Shack, 225 Two Lights Road, Cape Elizabeth, ME 04107. 207-799-1677.
http://lobstershacktwolights.com

J's Oyster Bar, 5 Portland Pier, Portland, ME 04102.
207-772-4828. *www.jsoyster.com*

Harraseeket Lunch and Lobster Company, 36 Main Street, South Freeport, ME 04078. 207-865-4888.
www.harraseeketlunchandlobster.com

Five Islands Lobster Company, 1447 Five Islands Road, Georgetown, ME 04548. 207-371-2990.
www.fiveislandslobster.com

Shaw's Fish and Lobster Wharf, 129 State Route 32, New Harbor, ME 04554. 207-677-2200.
www.shawswharf.com

Cod End Cookhouse, Commercial Street, Tenants Harbor, ME 04860. 207-372-6782. *www.codend.com*

Bagaduce Lunch, Frank's Flat Road (Route 176), Penobscot, ME 04476. 207-326-4197.

Tidal Falls Lobster Restaurant, (formerly of Hancock, ME) Tidal Falls Road (off Eastside Road), Hancock, ME 04640. 207-422-6457.

Thurston's Lobster Pound, 2 Steamboat Wharf Road, Bernard, ME 04612. 207-244-7600.
http://thurstonslobster.com

Massachusetts

The North Shore

Clam Box, 246 High Street, (Route 1A), Ipswich, MA 01938. 978-356-9707.
www.ipswichma.com/ipswichma/clambox

J.T. Farnham's, 88 Eastern Avenue (Route 133), Essex, MA 01929. 978-768-6643.

Woodman's of Essex, 121 Main Street (Route 133), Essex, MA 01929. 800-649-1773.
www.woodmans.com

Cape Cod and Martha's Vineyard

The Bite, 29 Basin Road, Menemsha (Martha's Vineyard), MA 02552. 508-645-9239.
www.thebitemenemsha.com

Captain Frosty's, 219 Route 6A, Dennis, MA 02638. 508-385-8548.
www.captainfrosty.com

Land Ho!, 38 Main Street (Route 6A) and Cove Road, Orleans, MA 02653. 508-255-5165.
www.land-ho.com

Tip For Tops'n, 31 Bradford Street, Provincetown, MA 02657. 508-487-1811.

New Hampshire

BG's Boat House Restaurant, 191 Wentworth Road (Route 1 B), Portsmouth, NH 03801. 603-431-1074.
www.bgsboathouse.com

Rhode Island

Aunt Carrie's, 1240 Ocean Road, (End of Route 108), Narragansett, RI 02882. 401-783-7930.
www.auntcarriesri.com

Champlin's Seafood, 256 Great Island Road, Narragansett, RI 02882. 401-783-3152.
www.champlins.com

Chopmist Charlie's, 40 Narragansett Avenue, Jamestown, RI 02835. 401-423-1020.
www.chopmistcharlies.com

Evelyn's Drive-In, 2335 Main Road, Tiverton, RI 02878. 401-624-3100.
www.evelynsdrivein.com

Flo's Clam Shack, 4 Wave Avenue, Middletown, RI 02842. 401-847-8141. Annex on Park Avenue, Island Park, Portsmouth, RI 02871.

Quito's Restaurant, 411 Thames Street, Bristol, RI 02809. 401-253-4500.
http://quitosrestaurant.com

Geographic Listing of Weekend Itineraries Stops

Profiled restaurants in italics; addresses at left.

Bristol, Rhode Island and Environs
Rhode Island and Massachusetts

Quito's Restaurant

Hope Diner, 742 Hope Street, Bristol, RI 02809

Evelyn's Drive-In

Gray's Ice Cream, 16 East Road, Tiverton, RI 02878

Flo's Clam Shack

Chopmist Charlie's

The Back Eddy, 1 Bridge Road, Westport, MA 02790

Aunt Carrie's

Champlin's Seafood

Iggy's Doughboys, 1157 Point Judith Road, Narragansett, RI 02882

Portland in the Rough
Maine

J's Oyster Bar

Becky's Diner, 390 Commercial Street, Portland, ME 04101

Harraseeket Lunch and Lobster

Maple's Organics Desserts, 14 Gary Maietta Parkway, South Portland, ME 04106

Smiling Hill Farm, 781 County Road, Westbrook, ME 04092

Two Lights Lobster Shack

Fore Street Restaurant, 288 Fore Street, Portland, ME 04101

Standard Baking Co., 75 Commercial Street, Portland, ME 04101

The Porthole, 20 Custom House Wharf, Portland, ME 04101

A Clam Alley Crawl
Massachusetts

Woodman's of Essex

The Lobster Pool 329 Granite Street, Rockport, MA 01966

Two Sisters, 27 Washington Street, Gloucester, MA 01930

Lee's, 2 East Main Street, Gloucester, MA 01930

The Dory, *closed*

Clam Box

J.T. Farnham's

White Farms Ice Cream, 326 High Street, Ipswich, MA 01938

Causeway Restaurant, 78 Essex Avenue, Gloucester, MA 01930

Village Restaurant, 55 Main Street, Essex, MA 01929

Credits

Photographs:
© Kindra Clineff: pages i, viii, ix, x, xii, 6, 25, 106, 108, 154, 166, 178, 190, 201, and 234.
© Kevin Kennefick: pages iv, 15, 47, 53, 55, 65, 91, and 156.
© Susan Capone Maloney: pages 36, 40, 141, and 168.
© Tim Peters Photography: page 23 bottom.
Giles Prett: pages 17, 30, 50, 188, and 197.

Publisher's Acknowledgments
The publisher gratefully acknowledges the contributions of individuals and establishments who helped make possible the art featured in *The New England Clam Shack Cookbook.*

Establishments featured in the book that provided photographs and/or ephemera:
Aunt Carrie's, Bagaduce Lunch, BG's Boat House Restaurant, The Bite, Captain Frosty's, Champlin's Seafood, Chopmist Charlie's, Clam Box, The Clam Shack, Cod End Cookhouse, Evelyn's Drive-In, Five Islands Lobster Company, Flo's Clam Shack, Harraseeket Lunch, J's Oyster Bar, J.T. Farnham's, Land Ho!, Lenny & Joe's Fish Tale, Maine Diner, Pearl Oyster Bar, The Place, Quito's Restaurant, Sea Swirl, Seahorse Tavern, Shaw's Fish and Lobster Wharf, Thurston's Lobster Pound, Tidal Falls Lobster Kettle, Tip For Tops'n, Two Lights Lobster Shack, and Woodman's of Essex.

Additional Photographers:
Deborah Balmuth, Deborah Burns, Rita Bloom, Brooke Dojny, Janet Harris, Janna Kohut, Cynthia McFarland, Wendy Palitz, Ilona and Jim Sherratt, and Kelly Suer.

Props:
Boston Seafood Restaurant, North Adams, Massachusetts; Drum Rock Products, Warwick, Rhode Island; and Fish Tales, Brooklyn, New York.

Resources

Mail-Order Sources

Cooks Shop Here
413-584-5116
www.cooksshophere.com
Panko crumbs and other hard-to-find
ingredients and specialty foods.

Drum Rock Products
401-737-5165
www.drumrockproducts.com
Wholesale source for Clam Fritter Batter Mix and Fis-
Chic Wonder Batter, an all-purpose breading and
batter mix. See website for places to purchase their
products.

Fiddler's Green Farm
800-729-7935
www.fiddlersgreenfarm.com
Finely milled corn flour.

Frank's RedHot
www.franksredhot.com
Reckitt Benckiser Inc.
Hot sauce preferred by some restaurants
in the book.

Gaspar's Sausage Company, Inc.
800-542-2038
www.linguica.com
Portuguese linguiça and chourico.

George's Place Fish Market
508-432-5493
www.georgesfishmarket.com
Seafood indigenous to Cape Cod, including
hard-shell and soft-shell clams, oysters, mussels,
scallops, and finfish such as cod, haddock,
and swordfish.

Hancock Gourmet Lobster Company
800-552-0142
www.hancockgourmetlobster.com
Mail-order everything lobster including lobster
stew, lobster roll makings, and even a complete
shore dinner.

Maine Lobster Direct
800-556-2783
www.mainelobsterdirect.com

Stonington Seafood
888-402-2729
www.stoningtonseafood.com
Smoked and fresh seafood including live
lobsters, crabmeat, scallops, and finfish
according to seasonal availability.

Whaler Seafood Specialties
508-996-3400
Mild or spicy baked stuffed quahogs.

Miscellaneous

Cabbage Island Clambakes
207-633-7200
www.cabbageislandclambakes.com
Hosts public clambakes.

Susan Herrmann Loomis
www.onruetatin.com
Cookbook author and proprietor
of On Rue Tatin cooking school.

Pearl Oyster Bar,
18 Cornelia Street,
New York, NY 10014.
212-691-8211
www.pearloysterbar.com
Open for lunch and dinner.

Index

Other Storey Titles You Will Enjoy